.1

Lombardo, Victor S.

Paraprofessionals
th young children:

+LB2844.1 .A8 L57

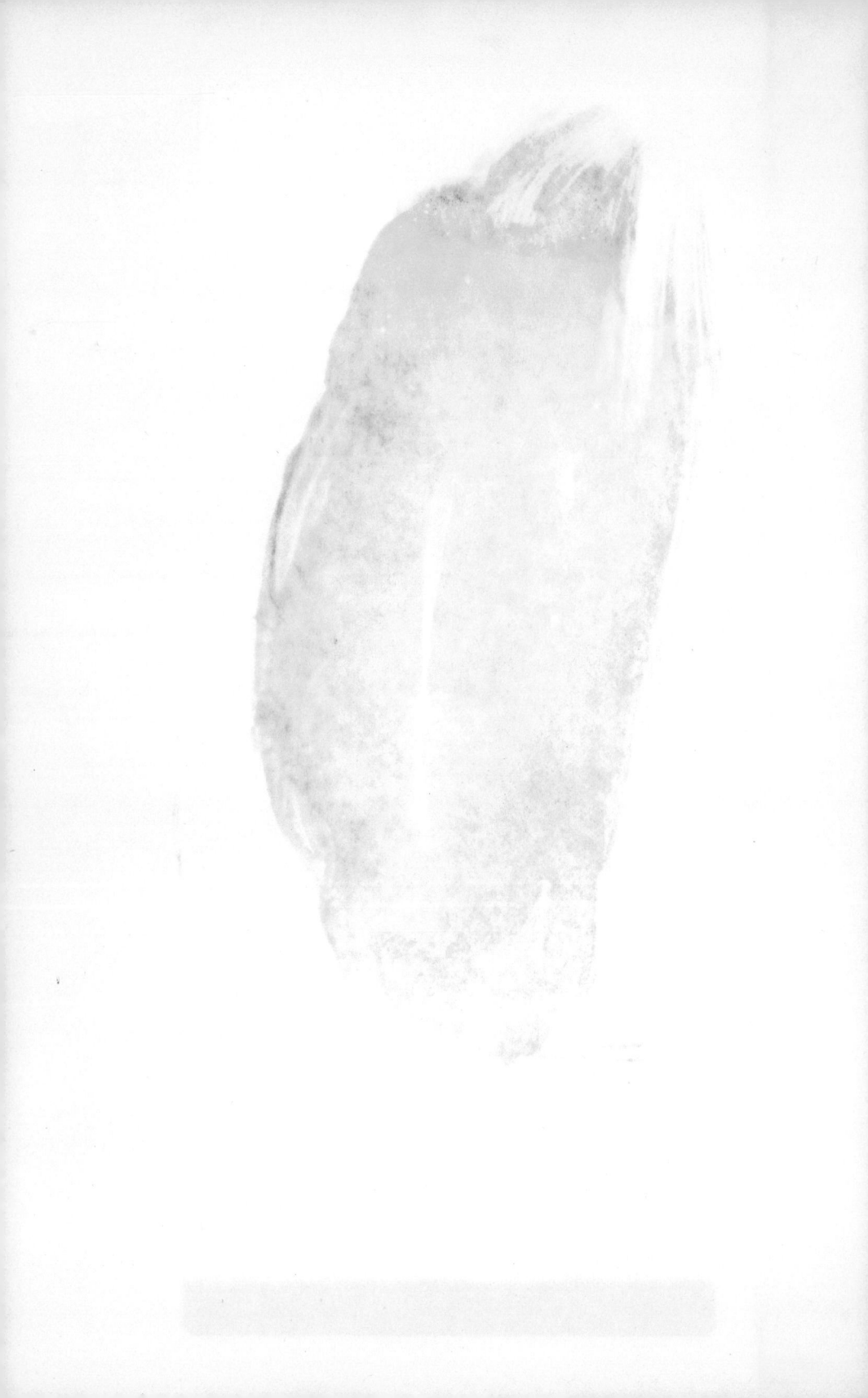

Pamphlets with Working
with Young Children

Paraprofessionals Working with Young Children

Paraprofessionals Working with Young Children

INFANCY THROUGH THE THIRD GRADE

By

VICTOR S. LOMBARDO, Ed.D.

Professor
Special Education Program
West Virginia College of Graduate Studies
Institute, West Virginia

CHARLES C THOMAS • PUBLISHER
Springfield • Illinois • U.S.A.

Published and Distributed Throughout the World by
CHARLES C THOMAS ● PUBLISHER
2600 South First Street
Springfield, Illinois, 62717, U.S.A.

This book is protected by copyright. No part of it may be reproduced in any manner without written permission from the publisher.

© *1981 by* CHARLES C THOMAS ● PUBLISHER
ISBN 0-398-04532-1
Library of Congress Catalog Card Number: 81-5690

With THOMAS BOOKS *careful attention is given to all details of manufacturing and design. It is the Publisher's desire to present books that are satisfactory as to their physical qualities and artistic possibilities and appropriate for their particular use.* THOMAS BOOKS *will be true to those laws of quality that assure a good name and good will.*

Printed in the United States of America
V-RX-1

Library of Congress Cataloging in Publication Data
Lombardo, Victor S.
  Paraprofessionals working with young children.

  Bibliography: p.
  Includes index.
  1. Teachers assistants. 2. Education, Primary. I. Title.
LB2844.1.A8L57   372.11'4124   81-5690
ISBN 0-398-04532-1   AACR2

*to my children
Victor, Michael
and Anthony
the best early childhood
instructors I ever had*

PREFACE

THE purpose of this text is to train paraprofessionals (aides, auxiliaries) to work with young children from infancy to age eight. In addition, it is intended to assist paraprofessionals working with young children in the following types of settings: (1) public school, (2) preschool/nursery school, and (3) day-care programs.

Paraprofessionals Working with Young Children: Infancy Through the Third Grade can be used as pre-service text by colleges and universities or as an in-service text by school districts, industry, as well as private and public organizations and agencies. This book provides important information regarding selected listings of developmental characteristics of particular age levels of young children on data compiled by the author.

The text is unique in that it takes rather technical research data and translates this information into nontechnical terms. In addition, each chapter is comprised of practical guidelines and suggestions that have actually been tested by the author, who has co-founded several early childhood programs and has served as a consultant to early childhood programs throughout the nation. It is hoped that the book will be enjoyed by teachers, parents, and other professionals, as well as paraprofessionals involved in the education and/or care of young children.

V.S.L.

ACKNOWLEDGMENTS

APPRECIATION is expressed to Dr. Daniel J. Kauffman, Dr. James E. Althof, Ms. Frances Fuller, Dr. Ruth V. Burgess, Dr. Joseph F. Stewart, Jr., and Ms. Jean Benish for their critical review of the original manuscript.

My sincerest thanks are expressed to my wife, Edith, for her support in allowing me to field-test training materials in several early childhood programs she directed and for providing valuable feedback.

Special thanks are expressed to Ms. Phyllis Bias for typing the final manuscript and to Ms. Lisa Nutter for typing certain sections of the original manuscript.

V.S.L.

CONTENTS

	Page
Preface	vii
Acknowledgments	ix

Chapter

1. PARAPROFESSIONALS WORKING WITH YOUNG CHILDREN: AN INTRODUCTION AND OVERVIEW 3
2. PARAPROFESSIONALS WORKING IN AN INFANT-TODDLER PROGRAM 29
3. PARAPROFESSIONALS WORKING IN A DAY-CARE AND/OR PRESCHOOL PROGRAM 55
4. PARAPROFESSIONALS WORKING IN A KINDERGARTEN PROGRAM 76
5. PARAPROFESSIONALS WORKING IN A FIRST-GRADE PROGRAM 95
6. PARAPROFESSIONALS WORKING IN A SECOND-GRADE PROGRAM 114
7. PARAPROFESSIONALS WORKING IN A THIRD-GRADE PROGRAM 133

Glossary 157
Author Index 159
Subject Index 161

Paraprofessionals Working
with Young Children

CHAPTER 1

PARAPROFESSIONALS WORKING WITH YOUNG CHILDREN: AN INTRODUCTION AND OVERVIEW

DESIRED LEARNER OUTCOMES

UPON completion of this chapter the paraprofessional will be able to:

- Define each of the following concepts and vocabulary words relative to early childhood education:
    affective development
    cognitive development
    day-care program
    developmental day-care program
    evening-care program
    motor development
    night-care program
    nursery school
    perceptual development
    physical development
    preschool program
    sensory development
    special child
- Identify the major levels of a Career Ladder Model showing the steps at which paraprofessionals enter the field.
- Identify similarities and differences between preschool, day-care and night-care programs.
- List and discuss events that have influenced the early childhood movement and the paraprofessional movement.
- List and discuss future projections relative to early childhood education programs and paraprofessionals working with young children.

INTRODUCTION

Today, the utilization of paraprofessionals working with young children ages infancy to eight years is a major trend in the field of early childhood education. There are 1.5 million paid paraprofessionals and 6 million unpaid paraprofessionals in the schools of our nation. In addition, there are more than 1 million paid and unpaid paraprofessionals working with young children in preschool, day-care, and other related early childhood programs in the United States. Although paraprofessionals working with young children include men and women, the majority are comprised of women.

Who Are the Paraprofessionals Working with Young Children?

A paraprofessional in a *preschool/nursery school program* is a person who assists the teacher in working with young children (3-5 years of age) in a variety of activities sponsored by the preschool and is supervised by the teacher.

A paraprofessional in an *early childhood public school program* also assists the teacher in working with young children (5-8 years of age) in a variety of activities in the classroom and in the school and is supervised by the teacher.

A paraprofessional in a *day-care program* is a person who assists the teacher/head caregiver in working with young children (infancy to 5 years of age) in a variety of activities provided by the program and is supervised by the teacher/head caregiver.

What Other Terms Are Used?

Paraprofessionals working with young children have been referred to by the following titles:

- child care volunteers
- day-care aides
- day-care assistants
- early childhood aides
- early childhood auxiliaries

CAREER LADDER MODEL

1) AIDE SUCH AS	**Illustrative Functions**	**Training Suggested**
GENERAL SCHOOL AIDE ...	Clerical, monitorial, custodial duties	Brief orientation period (2 or 3 weeks) in human development, social relations, and the school's goals and procedures, as well as some basic skill training
LUNCHROOM AIDE	Serving and preparation of food, monitorial duties	
TEACHER AIDE	Helping teacher in classroom, as needed	
FAMILY WORKER OR AIDE	Appointments, escorting, and related duties	
COUNSELOR AIDE	Clerical, receptionist, and related duties	no specified preschooling required.
LIBRARY AIDE	Helping with cataloging and distribution of books	
2) ASSISTANT SUCH AS	**Illustrative Functions**	**Training Suggested**
TEACHER ASSISTANT	More relationship to instructional process	High school diploma or equivalent; one year's inservice training or one year in college with practicum
FAMILY ASSISTANT	Home visits and organizing parent meetings	
COUNSELOR ASSISTANT ...	More work with records, listening to children sent from class to counselor's office because they are disrupting class	
LIBRARY ASSISTANT	More work with pupils in select books and reading to them	both can be on a work-study basis while working as an aide
3) ASSOCIATE SUCH AS	**Illustrative Functions**	**Training Suggested**
TEACHER ASSOCIATE	More responsibility with less supervision by the professional	A.A. degree from two-year college or two-year special program in a four-year college.
HOME-SCHOOL ASSOCIATE		
COUNSELOR ASSOCIATE ...		
LIBRARY ASSOCIATE		
SOCIAL WORK ASSOCIATE		both can be on work-study basis while working as an assistant
4) TEACHER-INTERN SUCH AS	**Illustrative Functions**	**Training Suggested**
STUDENT TEACHER	Duties very similar to those of associate but with more involvement in diagnosis and planning	B.A. or B.S. degree and enrollment in a college of teacher education or other institution which offers a program leading to a certification
STUDENT HOME-SCHOOL COORDINATOR		
STUDENT COUNSELOR		

5) TEACHER

Figure 1. POSSIBLE STAGES IN CAREER DEVELOPMENT OF AUXILIARIES. From G. W. Bowman and G. J. Klopf, *New Careers and Roles in the American School*. New York: Bank Street College, 1968. Reprinted by permission of Bank Street College.

- early childhood volunteers
- early education aides
- early education auxiliaries
- nursery school aides
- preschool assistants
- volunteer aides
- volunteer tutors

Professionals in the field are not always in agreement as to whether or not paraprofessionals are paid or unpaid workers. In some situations, paraprofessionals earn salaries and are entitled to fringe benefits similar to other staff personnel. In other situations, paraprofessionals volunteer their services. This book makes no distinction between paid paraprofessionals and those who volunteer their services.

What Kinds of Educational Training and Experiences Are Required of Paraprofessionals in Early Childhood Education?

Paraprofessionals working in early childhood programs, including day-care, preschool, and public school programs, have been known to possess a wide range of educational training and experiences. In fact, some paraprofessionals do not even have a high school diploma or its equivalent. Other paraprofessionals may have a college degree.

Although day-care, preschool, and public school requirements for paraprofessionals often vary from state to state and from program to program, there does appear to be a series of steps at which the paraprofessional enters the field. For example, G. W. Bowman and G. J. Klopf (1968) have developed a Career Ladder Model (*see* Figure 1) that reveals the steps at which an individual enters the field of education as a paraprofessional (the authors use the term "auxiliary").

The Career Ladder Model shows that there are four levels involved. The first level may be referred to as the *paraprofessional aide state*. Depending on the specific duties assigned, the paraprofessional working in a day-care, preschool, or public school program may be asked to perform clerical, monitorial, cataloging, and/or various kinds of activities in the center or classroom. For example, those paraprofessionals assigned as teacher aides would assist teachers in directly working with young children, perhaps in small groups consisting of two or three youngsters. The paraprofessional aide stage is the level at which those individuals with only a minimum of educational training or experience enter the field. Those trainees who enter the field at the first level generally receive two or three weeks of in-service training, which is another way of saying on-the-job training. It is important to keep in mind that specific educational requirements such as a high school diploma or equivalent are usually not stated at this entry level. It seems that most of the trainees who work with young children in day-care, preschool, and public school programs enter the field at the first level.

The second level of the career ladder may be referred to as the *paraprofessional assistant stage*. In this phase, trainees who enter the field usually have or are nearing completion of a high school diploma or equivalent and, in some instances, may be in the process of completing one year of college training. Although the paraprofessional at this stage may assume the same type of duties as those trainees at the first stage, they generally assume more duties and responsibilities in the day-care center, preschool, or public school classroom that are more directly related to teaching.

The next level may be referred to as the *paraprofessional associate stage*. Those trainees at this stage generally possess or are in the process of completing an associate of arts degree or two years of college training within a "four-year" college. Since trainees at this stage possess more educational training and experience than those in the first two levels, they are given more responsibility in the day-care center, preschool, or public school classroom with less supervision by the teacher.

The fourth level may be referred to as the *teacher-intern stage*. Individuals who enter at this stage are usually those persons pursuing a career as a professional teacher. Trainees at this level are often in the process of or have already completed a bachelor's degree from a four-year college, with certification in teacher education (early childhood education). Their responsibilities include duties that pertain to the actual planning of lessons for young children. Trainees at this level are still under the supervision of the professional in charge of the day-care program, preschool program, or early childhood public school program.

Trainees who enter the field either at the aide level, assistant level, associate level, or teacher-intern level are all considered to be paraprofessionals. This includes those employed by day-care programs, preschool programs, and early childhood public school programs, as well as those who volunteer their services.

What Is the Difference Between Preschool, Day-care and Night-care Programs?

Preschool is used interchangeably with the term "nursery school." Preschools generally provide educational programs that primarily center on the (1) cognitive, (2) affective, (3) sensory, (4) perceptual, (5) motor, and (6) physical development of young children. Before continuing, let us briefly look at each of the above terms with regard to the developmental characteristics of young children.

1. COGNITIVE DEVELOPMENT.* This concerns the degree to which the young child is able to acquire ideas by effectively utilizing mental processes and thinking skills.
2. AFFECTIVE DEVELOPMENT. This aspect of development deals with the overall personal, emotional, and social makeup of the young child.
3. SENSORY DEVELOPMENT. This is the level at which the young child is able to effectively utilize her/his senses. This includes the sense of sight, hearing, taste, smell, and touch.
4. PERCEPTUAL DEVELOPMENT. This aspect of development is concerned with the level at which the young child is able to assign meaning or understanding to information gained through the senses.
5. MOTOR DEVELOPMENT. This concerns the degree to which the young child is able to effectively utilize large muscles

---
*For purposes of this text, the author has decided to include language development characteristics together with cognitive development characteristics.

(gross motor) and small muscles (fine motor).
6. **PHYSICAL DEVELOPMENT.** This refers to the young child's growth in terms of height, weight, posture, and related areas.

Preschool programs generally provide services two to five days a week, half a day each time. Some have a half-day morning program for one group of preschoolers and a separate half-day afternoon program for another group of preschoolers.

Day-care is primarily an all-day child-care program for young children and provides child-care services five days a week. The terms "day-care," "quality day-care," and "developmental day-care" are often used interchangeably. It is important to remember that most day-care programs do include the major components of a preschool program; this means that it provides for the cognitive, affective, sensory, perceptual, motor, and physical development of young children. However, in addition, day-care programs generally provide for the nutritional, health, and other child-care needs of the young child when the parent is not present.

Some day-care programs also offer services to school-age children (age 6 and above) usually before and after school.

The terms "night-care program" and "evening-care program" are often used interchangeably. A night-care program is designed to provide child care at a child-care center in the evening and/or during the entire night. Night-care programs generally provide child-care services on a regular basis. It is interesting to note that, in many instances, night-care program requirements are often similar to those required of day-care programs. The Division of Family Services, or similar agency in your state, can usually provide specific information on night-care regulations and licensing requirements.

What Are the Historical Implications of the Early Childhood Education Movement and the Paraprofessional Movement?

Historically, we as a nation have always been interested in the welfare of young children (from birth to age 8). However, our nation's concern regarding the education of young children is a rather recent event. In support of this observation, G. S. Morrison (1976) reported:

> While we have always been interested to a greater or lesser extent in children, the most rapid growth in early childhood education has occurred from about 1965 to the present. It is only logical, therefore, that this is the period of time which has witnessed the greatest interest in young children in general and early childhood programs in particular.

This growing interest in young children and early childhood programs was brought about by several major events that occurred during the mid-to-late 1950s and 1960s. The first event focused upon the concern by professionals and others that the public schools of our nation were not properly teaching the basic skills subjects (reading, writing, and arithmetic). The second event concerned the fact that the Soviet Union launched the *Sputnik*. This sparked a national concern to take a closer look at our educational system. In particular, attention was directed at the need to provide worthwhile early childhood program opportunities for children of our nation. This attention was centered on improving the following conditions: (1) to reduce and eliminate the number of high school students who were unable to read or even perform related basic skills; and (2) to reduce and eliminate any gap between our nation's technology base and that of the Soviet Union by providing our citizens the advantage of early school opportunities.

National concern regarding poverty and its negative effects was another factor that sparked considerable interest in early childhood education. During the early 1960s our nation focused its attention on promoting early childhood education programs, with a special emphasis on serving those youngsters from low-income families. This was a time in our history when *Project Head Start* and other related antipoverty programs emerged.

A fourth factor that influenced early childhood education, during this time period, was the nationally recognized research work of certain researchers, especially Dr. Benjamin S. Bloom. According to Dr. Bloom (1964): "... in terms of intelligence measured at age 17, about 50% of the development takes place between conception and age 4, about 30% between 4 and 8, and about 20% between ages 8 and 17."

In other words, Dr. Bloom concluded that 80 percent of an individual's intellectual development occurs by the time the child reaches age eight. This research information gave dramatic support to professionals who voiced the need to provide early childhood education, especially during the child's first eight years of life. Some professionals argue that waiting to educate the young child at age six (the age in which formal schooling was provided) was too late, especially since 50 percent of intellectual development has already occurred by age four.

It is important to note that during this time an ever increasing number of women were entering the job market; this resulted in an increased need for child care. However, attention was directed at the need to provide child care, not education for these youngsters.

Parallel to this period of time, a number of experiments were being funded by the Ford Foundation to deal with another national concern. This concern focused upon the need to deal with the problem of overcrowded classrooms in order to allow teachers more time to teach, especially during a time when there was a shortage of certified teachers. The Ford Foundation sponsored the Bay City Project (Michigan), which is considered to be the first major experimental research study concerning the use of paraprofessionals in the schools. In addition, the Rutgers Study (New Jersey), the Newton Study (Massachusetts), the Yale-Fairfield Study (Connecticut), and numerous other research projects emerged. These studies dramatically revealed the beneficial effects of using paid and unpaid professionals in education in the schools, especially in the early grades when teacher-student ratios needed to be kept low.

During the 1960s several pieces of legislation were passed that provided federal funding for the training and utilization of paraprofessionals, including those programs involving paraprofessionals working with young children. Therefore, it should be rather easy to understand how the early childhood education movement, along with the paraprofessional movement, emerged as national priorities. In fact, the utilization of paraprofessionals in education, especially those programs in which paraprofessionals work with young children, is a major trend in the field today.

According to the professional literature, demands for early childhood programs in the United States with trained personnel, especially paraprofessionals, is here to stay. In other words, the need to train paraprofessionals to work with young children is not just a "passing fad" but a necessary and ongoing aspect of early childhood education programs.

Future Projections Relative to Early Childhood Education Programs and Paraprofessionals Working with Young Children

As already noted, paraprofessionals working with young children is currently a major trend in the field of education. It is anticipated that the following trends and issues will surface during the 1980s, with respect to early childhood education and the utilization of paraprofessionals with young children.

There Will Be a Continued Demand for Child-care Services for Young Children, Especially Those with Working Mothers

Today, women comprise 43 percent of the entire work force in the United States. Within the past four decades, the number of working women has increased twofold, and working women with children has increased tenfold. This means that the decade of the 1980s will witness the demand for child care, especially young children with working mothers.

It has been estimated that today there are approximately 7 million young children with working mothers, and the demand for child-care services by trained professionals and paraprofessionals is increasing every day. In fact, some experts predict that by the early 1990s there will be between 12-14 million young children with working mothers. In other words, child-care programs with trained professionals and paraprofessionals will continue to be in demand.

Private Industry Will Increasingly Sponsor Day-care and Night-care Programs for the Children of Their Employees

Industry is beginning and will continue to take a leadership role in sponsoring child-care programs for the young children of their employees. These programs are often staffed with trained professionals and paraprofessionals. Company-sponsored child-care services have been beneficial to employees and employers alike. Those companies that have already begun to provide child-care services report the following benefits of such programs:

1. Employees tend to feel better about their jobs in knowing that their young children are being cared for while they are working.
2. Employees often feel more secure in knowing that they are in close proximity of their young child should any emergencies or needs arise.
3. Employees who like the company in which they are employed are less likely to find employment somewhere else. Often the result is a substantial reduction in employee turnover.
4. Employees who bring their youngsters to work and leave them at a company-sponsored child-care center are less likely to be late for work.
5. Employees who have their youngsters in company-sponsored child-care programs are less likely to be absent from work.
6. Employees can spend time with their children during lunch period. This is beneficial to the child as well as the parent(s).

One nationally recognized company-sponsored child-care program is the Stride Rite® Children's Center in Boston, Massachusetts. It is interesting to note that this company-sponsored day-care program serves its employees and members of the neighboring community. A floor plan (*see* Figure 2) and a playground plan (*see* Figure 3) is provided for this industrial/community day-care center. This program includes a staff of

Day Care Center floor plan

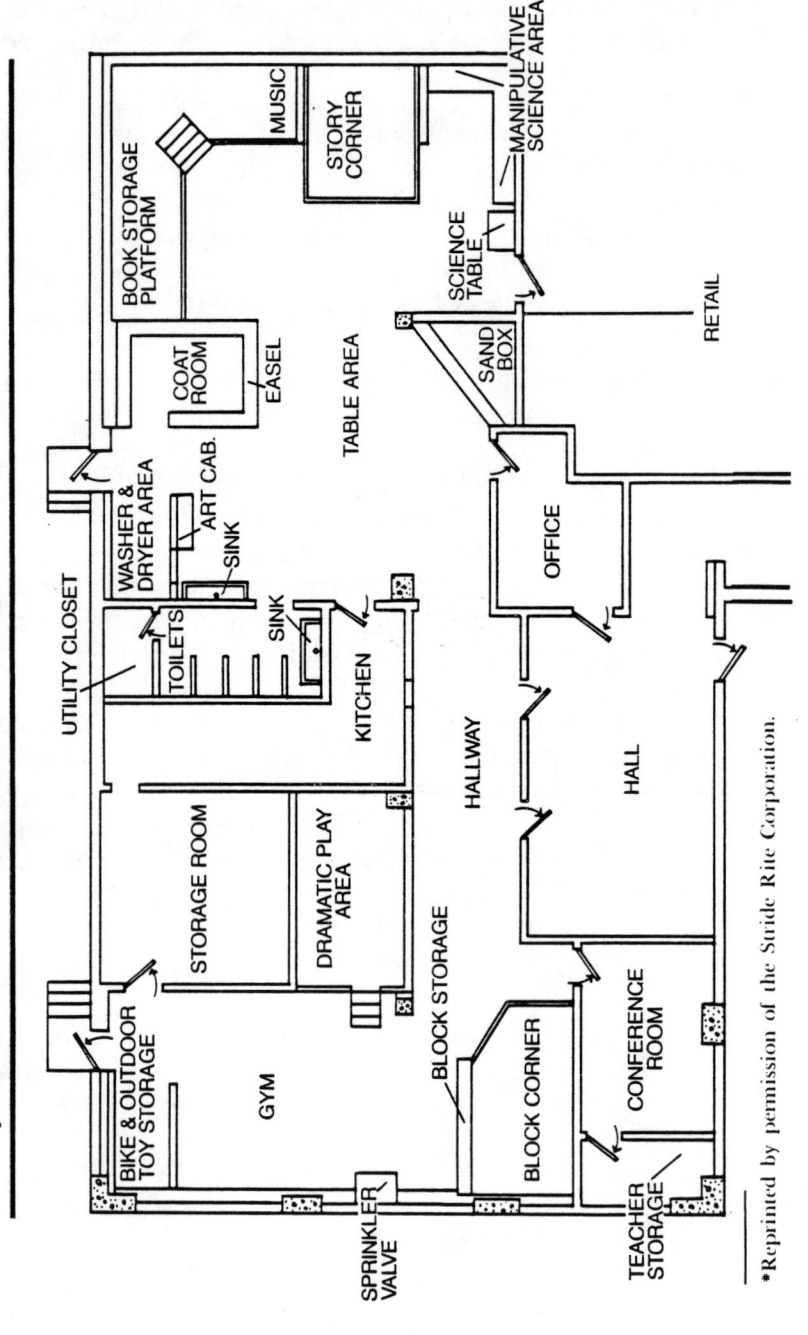

*Reprinted by permission of the Stride Rite Corporation.

Figure 2. Plan of day-care center. (Copyright Stride Rite Corporation, 1977 [H.F. Gamarsh].)

Day Care Center playground

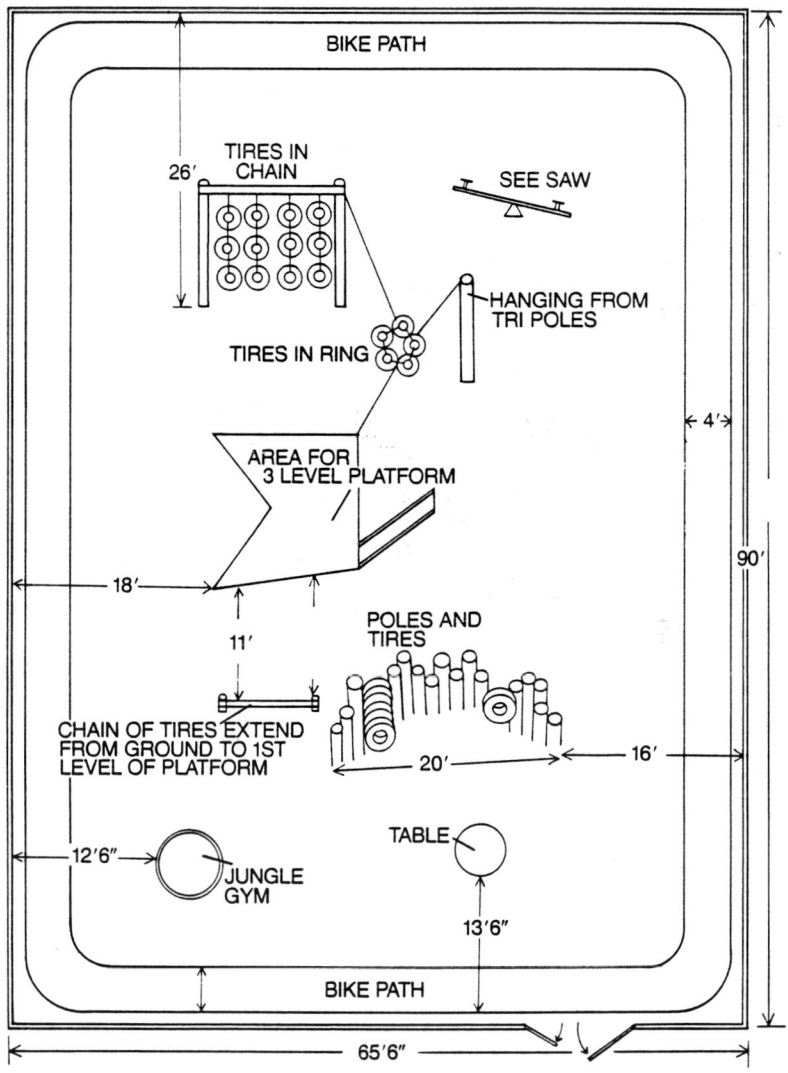

*Reprinted by permission of the Stride Rite Corporation.

Figure 3. Day-care center playground. (Copyright Stride Rite Corporation, 1975 [Bob Plocharceyk].)

trained professionals and paraprofessionals.

There Will Be an Increased Interest on the Part of State Agencies to Develop Specific Procedures for the Certification of Paraprofessionals

J. M. Hale and C. Ulmer (1972) provides a series of important reasons why state certification is important:

1. Order can be brought to a potentially "chaotic" situation by creating a comprehensive set of certification guidelines.
2. The existence of these guidelines will lead to increased status for the paraprofessional movement.
3. Additional career opportunities will be provided for citizens within the state.
4. An adequate foundation for paraprofessionals utilization and advancement will be created, which, in turn, will encourage local school districts to consider adoption of programs consistent with the state policy.
5. The children and youth in the schools will, as a result of additional personnel, be the beneficiaries of improved and more individualized instruction.*

There Will Be Continued Demand for Preschool Intervention Programs for Young Children from Low-income Families

A decade ago a number of professionals were critical of Head Start and similar preschool intervention programs for youngsters for low-income families. Some professionals argued that any possitive effects of preschool intervention disappeared in a year or two after the child attended such a program.

However, a recent comprehensive follow-up report of the long-term effects of Head Start and related programs reveals that these programs are highly beneficial to youngsters from low-income families. In fact, Drs. Irving Lazar and Richard Darlington (1979), of Cornell University, in their research report concluded that early education programs for low-income children exert the following long-term effects:

---
*From the book, *Administrator's Guide To Training Paraprofessionals* by J.M. Hale and C. Ulmer© 1972 by Prentice-Hall, Inc., Englewood Cliffs, New Jersey 07632

1. Early intervention programs dramatically decreased the number of children classified as "special" and then placed in a special education program. A special child is one who deviates from the "normal" in terms of cognitive, sensory, perceptual, motor, physical, and/or affective developmental characteristics to such a degree that s/he may need specialized materials, equipment, and/or services.
2. Early intervention programs markedly decreased the number of children "held back" or retained in grade.
3. The achievement scores of low-income children who attended early intervention programs appreciably increased, especially in the areas of reading and math.
4. Low-income children who attended preschools also exhibited higher scores on test of intelligence, as a result of early intervention programs.
5. A substantial number of low-income youngsters who attended preschools were more prone to feel good about themselves and their own individual accomplishments.

The professional literature is increasingly revealing the need for providing early intervention programs with trained personnel, especially paraprofessionals. This, in turn, will require more early intervention programs to hire fully trained paraprofessionals and/or provide comprehensive in-service, on-the-job training of their own.

Paraprofessionals Will Be Increasingly Called upon to Work with Young Handicapped Children

The author in a previous book, *Paraprofessionals in Special Education* (1980) reported that:

> The professional literature reveals that in the future, trained paraprofessionals in special education are especially critical in carrying our provisions of PL 94-142 pertaining to early childhood education programs. This means that training programs during the 1980's will have to provide additional instruction pertaining to specific techniques that paraprofessionals should be able to use effectively in working with young children.

Public Law 94-142 is another name for the Education of All Handicapped Children Act of 1975. This federal law represents one of the most comprehensive pieces of legislation in the history of our nation pertaining to the education of special students.

As states continue to carry out the requirements of PL 94-142, especially with regard to providing free and appropriate education for handicapped students, including young handicapped children, there will be a continued need to utilize trained paraprofessionals. In support of this observation, J. Harvey (1976) indicated that: "For some time, the assistance of volunteers has been important in employing tutorial and small group strategies in serving handicapped children and for the future, it could be critical in implementing provisions of the law dealing with early childhood education and programs for the severely handicapped."

In other words, paraprofessionals working with young special children and normal young children will continue to remain in the forefront throughout the decade of the 1980s and the early 1990s.

Institutions of Higher Education Will Be Increasingly Asked to Train Paraprofessionals to Work in a Variety of Settings with Young Children

Two-year community colleges and four-year colleges and universities in the nation will increasingly be called upon to provide pre-service and in-service (on-the-job) training programs designed to prepare paraprofessionals to work with young children in public school, preschool/nursery, and day-care programs. These institutions of higher education will be required to work more cooperatively with school districts and private industry, as well as public and private agencies and organizations concerned with utilizing trained paraprofessionals to work with young children. (For a listing of selected agencies and organizations concerned with young children, see Appendix B of this chapter.)

SUMMARY

The utilization of paraprofessionals working with young children (infancy to 8 years of age) is a major trend in the field of early childhood education. It was estimated that 1.5 million paid paraprofessionals and 6 million unpaid paraprofessionals are serving in the schools of our nation. Also, approximately 1 million paid and unpaid paraprofessionals work with young children in preschool, day-care, and other related early childhood programs in the United States.

Terms used interchangeably with the term "paraprofessional" were provided.

A career ladder was presented that revealed that paid and unpaid paraprofessionals enter the field at any one of four levels: (1) aide level; (2) assistant level; (3) associate level; and (4) teacher-intern level.

Similarities and differences between day-care and night-care programs were presented.

A brief overview of the historical implications of the early childhood education movement and the paraprofessional movement was provided. Attention was directed at major events that occurred during the mid-to-late 1950s, 1960s.

Future projections relative to early childhood education programs and paraprofessionals working with young children were presented. These projections indicated that the utilization of trained paraprofessionals to work with young children is a national priority and will continue to remain in the forefront throughout the decade of the 1980s and the early 1990s.

APPENDIX A

Chapter Review

The following sample questions are designed to assist the paraprofessional in reviewing information presented in this chapter. The answer key is located at the end of this appendix. (*Note*: Training supervisors may decide to add questions of their own, based on local needs.)

Multiple-choice Questions

1. The first level of the Career Ladder Model presented in this chapter is the:
   ( ) A. Paraprofessional assistant stage
   ( ) B. Paraprofessional aide stage
   ( ) C. Paraprofessional assoicate stage
   ( ) D. Teacher-intern stage
2. Paraprofessionals working with young children have been referred to by which of the following:
   ( ) A. Early childhood aides
   ( ) B. Early childhood auxiliaries
   ( ) C. Both A and B are correct
   ( ) D. None of the above are correct
3. Today, women comprise approximately what percentage of the entire work force in the nation?
   ( ) A. 43%
   ( ) B. 90%
   ( ) C. 14%
   ( ) D. 34%
4. The area of development that deals with the overall personal emotional and social makeup of the young child is:
   ( ) A. Cognitive development
   ( ) B. Affective development
   ( ) C. Sensory development
   ( ) D. None of the above are correct
5. The third level of the Career Ladder Model presented in this chapter is the:
   ( ) A. Teacher-intern stage

( ) B. Paraprofessional associate stage
( ) C. Paraprofessional assistant stage
( ) D. All the above are correct
6. Paraprofessionals, as defined in this text, include:
( ) A. Paid workers only
( ) B. Unpaid workers only
( ) C. Both paid and unpaid workers
( ) D. None of the above are correct
7. The area of development that deals with the degree to which the young child is able to acquire ideas by effectively utilizing mental processes and thinking skills is:
( ) A. Physical development
( ) B. Affective development
( ) C. Sensory development
( ) D. Cognitive development
8. According to Dr. Benjamin S. Bloom, what percentage of an individual's intellectual development occurs by the time the child reaches age four?
( ) A. 50
( ) B. 90
( ) C. 70
( ) D. 80
9. By the early 1990s, there will be between how many million young children in the nation with working mothers?
( ) A. 2-4
( ) B. 120-125
( ) C. 12-14
( ) D. 3-6
10. Which of the following does *not* pertain to the paraprofessional aide stage of the Career Ladder Model?
( ) A. Most trainees enter at this level
( ) B. Most trainees have a bachelor's degree
( ) C. Minimum of educational training is required
( ) D. Minimum of educational experience is required
11. According to Dr. Benjamin S. Bloom, about what percentage of an individuals' intellectual development occurs by the time the child reaches age eight?
( ) A. 80
( ) B. 90

      ( ) C. 100
      ( ) D. None of the above are correct
12. Which term is used interchangeably with the term "night care"?
      ( ) A. Preschool
      ( ) B. Nursery school
      ( ) C. Evening care
      ( ) D. None of the above are correct
13. Which of the following represent major events occurring during the mid-to-late 1950s and 1960s that have historically influenced the early childhood movement?
      ( ) A. *Sputnik* launching
      ( ) B. Concern about the number of high school students not able to read
      ( ) C. Negative effects of poverty
      ( ) D. All the above are correct
14. Company-sponsored child-care programs have been beneficial in which of the following ways?
      ( ) A. Employee turnover is often reduced
      ( ) B. Absenteeism tends to be reduced
      ( ) C. Employees are less likely to be late for work
      ( ) D. All the above are correct
15. Which terms is used interchangeably with the term "developmental day-care"?
      ( ) A. Quality day-care
      ( ) B. Preschool care
      ( ) C. Nursery school care
      ( ) D. None of the above are correct

True/False Questions

    T   F
1. ( ) ( ) Perceptual development concerns the level at which the young child is able to assign meaning to information gained through the senses.
2. ( ) ( ) The Bay City Project is considered to be the first major experimental research study concerning the use of paraprofessionals in the schools.
3. ( ) ( ) According to this text, day-care is primarily a

Working with Young Children

half-day child-care program for young children.

4. ( ) ( ) *Preschool* is often used interchangeably with the term "nursery school."

5. ( ) ( ) The second level of the Career Ladder Model presented in this chapter is the Paraprofessional assistant stage.

6. ( ) ( ) According to Dr. Benjamin S. Bloom, about 100 percent of intellectual development occurs by age four.

7. ( ) ( ) Today, there are approximately 7 million young children with working mothers.

8. ( ) ( ) A special child is one who deviates from the "normal" in terms of cognitive, sensory, perceptual, motor, physical, or affective developmental characteristics to such a degree that s/he may need specialized materials, equipment, and/or services.

9. ( ) ( ) Sensory development refers to the level at which the young child is able to effectively utilize her/his senses.

10. ( ) ( ) The majority of paraprofessionals working with young children are men.

11. ( ) ( ) Trainees who enter the field either at the aide level, assistant level, associate level, or teacher-intern level are considered to be paraprofessionals.

12. ( ) ( ) According to Drs. Irving Lazar and Richard Darlington in their research report, early intervention programs for low-income children markedly decreased the number of children "held back" or retained in grade.

13. ( ) ( ) Public Law 94-142 is another name for the Education For All Handicapped Children Act of 1975.

14. ( ) ( ) Within the past forty years, the number of working women with children has increased tenfold.

15. ( ) ( ) Most of the trainees enter the field at the paraprofessional associate stage.

Answer Key

Answer to Multiple-choice Questions

1. B
2. C
3. A
4. B
5. B
6. C
7. D
8. A
9. C
10. B
11. A
12. C
13. D
14. D
15. A

Answers to True/False Questions

1. True
2. True
3. False
4. True
5. True
6. False
7. True
8. True
9. True
10. False
11. True
12. True
13. True
14. True
15. False

APPENDIX B

Selected Listing of Agencies and Organizations Concerned with Young Children

Name: American Association of Elementary — Kindergarten — Nursery Educators
1201 — 16th Street
Washington, D. C. 20036

Name: Association for Childhood Education International
3615 Wisconsin Avenue, N. W.
Washington, D. C. 20016

Name: Child Welfare League of America, Inc.
44 East 23rd Street
New York, New York 10010

Name: Day Care and Child Development Council of America, Inc.
1401 K. Street. N. W.
Washington, D. C. 20005

Name: Educational Resources Information Center/Early Childhood Education
805 West Pennsylvania Avenue
Urbana, Illinois 61801

Name: National Association for the Education of Young Children
1834 Connecticut Avenue, N. W.
Washington, D. C. 20009

APPENDIX C

Suggested Readings and Films

Early Childhood Education

Almy, M. *Early Childhood Educator at Work*. New York: McGraw-Hill Book Company, 1975.
Cohen, D. J., and Brandegee, A. S. *Day Care: 3 Serving Preschool Children*. Washington, D. C.: Dept. of H. E. W. publication, 1974.
Hendrick, J. *The Whole Child: New Trends in Early Education*. Saint Louis: The C. V. Mosby Company, 1975.
Hildebrand, V. *Guiding Young Children*. New York: Macmillan Publishing Company, Inc., 1975.
Jordan, J. B., and Darley, R. F. *Not all Little Red Wagona are Red: The Exceptional Child's Early Years*. Arlington, Virginia: The Council For Exceptional Children, 1973.
Morrison, G. S. *Early Childhood Education Today*. Columbus, Ohio: Charles E. Merrill Publishing Company, 1976.

Paraprofessionals

Bennet, W. S., Jr., and Falk, R. F. *New Careers and Urban Schools: A Sociological Study of Teacher Aide Roles*. New York: Holt, Rinehart and Winston, 1970.
Bowman, G. W., and Klopf, G. J. *New Careers and Roles in the American School*. New York: Bank Street College of Education for the Office of Economic Opportunity, 1968.
Bruner, C. A lap to sit on — and much more. *Childhood Education*, 43:20-23, 1962.
Emmerling, F. C., and Kanawha, Z. C. Innovations in Education: The Teacher Aide. *Education Leadership*, 24:175-184, 1966.
Greer, J. V. Utilizing Paraprofessionals and Volunteers in Special Education. *Focus on Exceptional Children* 10:1-15, 1978.
Lombardo, V. *Paraprofessionals in Special Education*. Springfield, Illinois: Charles C Thomas, Publisher, 1980.
Todd, V. E., and Hunter, G. H. *The Aide in Early Childhood Education*. New York: Macmillan Publishing Company, Inc., 1973.

Suggested Films

Film Title: "The Precious Years" (color)
Time: 30 minutes

Publisher: ABC Merchandising, Inc.
New York, New York 10036
Address: 1330 Avenue of The Americas
Film Title: "Setting the Stage for Learning" (color)
Time: 22 minutes
Publisher: Churchill Films
Address: 662 North Robertson Boulevard
Los Angeles, California 90069

REFERENCES

Almy, M. *Early Childhood Educator at Work.* New York: McGraw-Hill Book Company, 1975.

Bennett, W. S., Jr., and Falk, R. F. *New Careers and Urban Schools: A Sociological Study of Teacher Aide Roles.* New York: Holt, Rinehart and Winston, 1970.

Bloom, B. S. *Stability and Change in Human Characteristics.* New York: John Wiley and Sons, Inc., 1964, p. 88.

Bowman, G. W., and Klopf, G. J. *New Careers and Roles In The American School.* New York: Bank Street College of Education for the Office of Economic Opportunity, 1968.

Bruner, C. A lap to sit on — and much more. *Childhood Education, 43*:20-23, 1962.

Cohen, D. J., and Brandegee, A. S. *Day Care: 3 Serving Preschool Children.* Washington, D. C.: Dept. of H. E. W. Publicaiton 1974.

Emmerling, F. C., and Kanawha, Z. C. Innovation in Education: the teacher aide. *Education Leadership 24*:175-184, 1966.

Greer, J. V. Utilizing Paraprofessionals and volunteers in special education. *Focus On Exceptional Children, 10*:1-15, 1978.

Hale, J. M., and Ulmer, C. *Administrator's Guide to Training Paraprofessionals.* Englewood Cliffs, New Jersey: Prentice-Hall, 1972, p. 19.

Harvey, J. Future trends in personnel preparation. *Exceptional Children, 43*: 148-150, 1976.

Hendrick, J. *The Whole Child: New Trends in Early Education.* Saint Louis: The C. V. Mosby Company, 1975.

Hildebrand, V. *Guiding Young Children.* New York: Macmillan Publishing Company, Inc., 1975.

Jordan, J. B. and Darley, R. F. *Not all Little Red Wagons are Red: The Exceptional Child's Early Years.* Arlington, Virginia: The Council For Exceptional Children, 1973.

Lazar, I., and Darlington, R. "Summary Report: Lasting Effects After Preschool," Washington, D. C.: U. S. Administration for Children, Youth and Families (ACYF), 1979.

Lombardo, V. *Paraprofessionals in Special Education.* Springfield, Illinois: Charles C Thomas, Publisher, 1980, pp. 28-29.

Morrison, G. S. *Early Childhood Education Today.* Columbus, Ohio: Charles E. Merrill Publishing Company, 1976, pp. 2-3.

Todd, V. E. and Hunter, G. H. *The Aide in Early Childhood Education.* New York: Macmillan Publishing Company, Inc., 1973.

CHAPTER 2

PARAPROFESSIONALS WORKING IN AN INFANT-TODDLER PROGRAM

DESIRED LEARNER OUTCOMES

UPON completion of this chapter the paraprofessional will be able to:
- Define each of the following concepts and vocabulary words relative to early childhood education:
  center-based program
  CFRP
  home-based program
  home- and center-based program
  infant-toddler program
  self-help skills
- Identify and discuss major types of programs in which a paraprofessional works with infants and toddlers.
- List and discuss cognitive, affective, sensory, perceptual, motor, and physical developmental characteristics of infants and toddlers.
- Identify instructional and noninstructional activities in which a paraprofessional works with infants and toddlers.
- Identify major guidelines for a paraprofessional to follow when working with infants and toddlers.

Infant-toddler programs are usually designed for young children from birth to age three. This chapter briefly focuses on three types of programs in which a paraprofessional works with infants and toddlers: (1) a center-based program; (2) a home-based program; and (3) a home- and center-based program. Paraprofessionals who work in any of these programs for infants and toddlers enter the field at any one of the levels described in the Career Ladder Model (*see* Figure 1). Men as well as women work in infant-toddler programs, however, the majority are women.

Although residential (institutional) programs for infant and toddler orphans have existed for quite some time, the concept of caring for groups of infants and/or toddlers (other than orphaned children) by someone other than the child's parents or guardians for part of a day is a rather recent development in the United States.

It is important to note that the recent research findings of Drs. Lazar and Darlington (see Chapter 1) revealed the beneficial long-term effects of preschool programs, including programs serving infants and toddlers from low-income families.

The first type of program in which the paraprofessional may work with infants and toddlers are *center-based programs*.

Center-based programs are those in which the young child is cared for at a given facility. According to W. S. Hooks (1977): "Center-based care for infants and toddlers is in the pioneering state in this country. One of our oldest infant care centers, The Children's Center at Syracuse University, dates from 1964."

A review of the professional literature reveals that, historically, professionals have not been in universal agreement as to the merits of group care for infants and toddlers. In particular, their arguments in the past and to the present time have centered on the negative effects of residential-type infant and toddler group-care programs for orphans. In addition, some professionals point out that infants and toddlers who are not orphaned should be cared for at home exclusively by the mother, father, or legal guardian.

Today, an increasing number of professionals are reporting the positive effects of group care for infants and toddlers. In support of this position, M. E. Keister (1973) reported on the beneficial effects of group care for infants and toddlers. According to Dr. Keister, the intelligence test scores for infants and toddlers cared in group settings were higher in comparison to youngsters cared for at home.

E. B. Evans and G. E. Saia (1972) provide additional support regarding the merits of group care for infants and toddlers. They make the following conclusions: "... quality infant day care is not only a valuable supplement to exclusive home care, but in fact may be an improvement over typical home care because it stimulates an infant's physical, emotional, social, and intellectual development."

A second type of program in which the paraprofessional may work with infants and toddlers are *home-based programs*. Home-based programs are those in which care for infants and toddlers is provided in the young child's home. Home-based programs for infants and toddlers are also a rather recent development. One nationally recognized home-based program for infants and toddlers is the Florida Home Visitor Program. According to I. J. Gordon (1975):

> The basic program consisted of a once a week home visit by a paraprofessional parent educator, who was recruited from the same background as the mother and who had received special pre-service and continuous in-service training. At each visit, she presented the mother with an activity from a set of sequenced materials appropriate for the level of development of the child and demonstrated the activity. In addition, she showed the mother ways to make toys and mobiles from materials in the home. The activities from the age range 3 months to 24 months did not require store-bought materials.

A third type of program in which the paraprofessional may work with infants and toddlers is a *home- and center-based program*. In this type of program the paraprofessional generally works with the parent and child at the child's home and at a weekly center-based program as well.

There is a relatively new, federally funded, child-centered family services program referred to as the *Child and Family Resource Program* (CFRP). CFRP is designed to focus on the continuous needs of young children (prenatal period to age 8) and their entire family, particularly low-income families. Services include (1) early childhood education, (2) parent involvement, (3) health, and (4) family social services.

The CFRP of Bismark, North Dakota is a nationally recognized home- and center-based program for infants and toddlers. A brief description of this program follows: "In addition to the home-based educational program, parents and young children attended a weekly center-based program. This program includes shared activities between the parent and child, such as with storytelling and puppets. Center-based programs also include time for parent group meetings, which may include a discussion of mutual problems and workshops on child development and nutrition." (Early Childhood and Family Development Programs Improve the Quality of Low-Income Families, 1979.)

Whether the paraprofessional works in a center-based program, home-based program, or home- and center-based program, s/he must be knowledgeable of basic developmental characteristics of infants and toddlers. The following represents a selected listing of cognitive, affective, sensory, perceptual, motor, and physical developmental characteristics that are often observed in young children (birth to age three years). It is in no way intended to serve as an exhaustive listing. Although developmental characteristics often overlap with one another, and not all infants and toddlers develop at the exact same rate — as a group, young children tend to exhibit the following characteristics along approximate age ranges.

Cognitive Development

Between the time period from birth to four months the young child tends to exhibit the following characteristics:

- Shows interest in her/his own personal needs such as feeding (for example, cries when hungry).
- Shows interest in her/his own personal needs to be kept dry (for example, cries when wet).
- Shows interest in her/his own needs to be kept clean (for example, cries when diaper is soiled).
- Has established her/his own personal feeding time preferences (or routines).
- Has established her/his own personal sleeping time preferences (or routines).
- Makes vocal sounds in addition to crying.

Between the time period from 5-8 months the young child tends to exhibit the following characteristics:

- Enjoys babbling to herself/himself.
- Babbles in the company of others.
- Begins to imitate sounds of a familiar person.
- Able to say "da-da" or "ma-ma" (not aware of the meaning).

Working in an Infant-Toddler Program   33

- Tries to locate toys (objects) s/he hides in the crib or nearby.

Between the time period of 9-12 months the young child tends to exhibit the following characteristics:

- Able to say "da-da" or "ma-ma" (assigns meaning to one particular individual).
- Responds when her/his name is called.
- Likes looking at pictures in a book.
- Imitates more sounds of a familiar person.
- Imitates more gestures of a familiar person.

Between the time period from 13-16 months the young child tends to exhibit the following characteristics:

- Able to point to one or two of her/his own body parts.
- Able to follow a simple (one-part) direction, such as "Get Your Teddy."
- Able to call two or three persons by their name.
- Able to call a few objects by their name.

Between the time period from 17-20 months the young child tends to exhibit the following characteristics:

- Able to point to three or four of her/his own body parts.
- Able to call more persons by their name.
- Able to call more objects or toys by their name.
- Can follow more simple (one-part) directions.

Between the time period from 21-24 months the young child tends to exhibit the following characteristics:

- Able to point to her/his own body parts.
- Speaks in sentences using two words, such as "I go," or "I want."
- Enjoys experimenting with objects, such as a stick becomes a "gun."

Between the time period from 25-36 months the young child tends to exhibit the following characteristics:

- Speaks in sentences using two or three words, such as "See my truck."
- Can identify her/his full name.
- Can tell you the functions of parious body parts, such as

"Eat with mouth."
- Can learn simple games, such as "Ring Around The Rosey."
- Can learn simple songs, such as "Row, Row, Row Your Boat."

The time period from birth to age 36 months is a dramatic growth period in the life of a young child, especially in terms of cognitive or intellectual development. As already pointed out in Chapter 1, this is the period of time in which a substantial amount of intellectual development is observed.

Paraprofessionals working with children during this age range will note that it is a time span that begins with the infant having others doing most of her/his "thinking" for her/him to a young toddler (who reaches the age of 3) who wants to think for herself/himself.

Affective Development

Between the time period from birth to four months the young child tends to exhibit the following characteristics:
- Smiles when you play with her/him.
- Laughs when you play with her/him.
- Initiates smiling.
- Initates laughing.
- Responds favorably to personal contact.
- Likes to be held and cuddled.

Between the time period from 5-8 months the young child tends to exhibit the following characteristics:
- Enjoys playing "Peek-a-Boo."
- Laughs when a familiar person enters the room.
- Cries when a familiar person leaves the room.
- Enjoys personal contact for longer periods of time (pulls your hand, hair, etc.).
- Enjoys time alone with a favorite toy or object.

Between the time period from 9-12 months the young child tends to exhibit the following characteristics:
- The child is able to respond to the negative tone ("No") of

your voice.
- The child is able to respond to the positive tone ("Yes") of your voice.
- The child enjoys playing "Pat-a-Cake" with a familiar person.
- The child enjoys waving "bye-bye" to a familiar person.

Between the time period from 13-16 months the young child tends to exhibit the following characteristics:

- Sometimes appears stubborn and set in doing something her/his way.
- Exhibits a sense of humor.
- Enjoys playing near another child (not the same as playing with another child).

Between the time period from 17-20 months the young child tends to exhibit the following characteristics:

- Enjoys the company of others for longer periods of time.
- Often looks to adults s/he knows for approval.
- Openly shows her/his affection towards other children.
- Openly shows her/his affection towards adults s/he knows.

Between the time period from 21-24 months the young child tends to exhibit the following characteristics:

- Finds it difficult to share things (toys) with others.
- Frequently does just the opposite of what s/he was asked to do.
- Sometimes hits other children without any apparent reason.

Between the time period from 25-36 months a young child tends to exhibit the following characteristics:

- Enjoys using the pronouns "I" or "Me" to refer to her/him.
- Still enjoys playing next to another child and will play with another for only a short period of time.
- Takes pride in her/his accomplishment, such as showing you a completed finger painting and saying, "See my picture."

36   *Paraprofessionals Working with Young Children*

The time span from birth to age 36 months also indicates a substantial growth period pertaining to the young child's affective development. It is a time when the child learns new and exciting things about herself/himself. When making references to the development of young children two to three years of age, M. A. Stant (1972) stated: "He is still in the me-stage, striving to learn more about himself and his place in the social structure. After he learns about himself, he will be ready to extend his social living and work and play to others."

Sensory and/or Perceptual Development

Between the time period from birth to four months the young child tends to exhibit the following characteristics:

- Responds to sounds in the immediate environment.
- Responds to motion in the immediate environment.
- Can visually follow a moving object.

Between the time period from 5-8 months the young child tends to exhibit the following characteristics:

- Explores her/his environment by touching nearby objects.
- Explores her/his environment by tasting nearby objects.
- Responds to brightly colored objects.
- Turns her/his head toward the person speaking.
- Spends more time looking at new objects (toys).

Between the time period from 9-12 months the young child tends to exhibit the following characteristics:

- Able to feed herself/himself small morsels of food.
- Attempts to eat with a spoon (smears more than s/he eats).
- Likes to dump things out of containers and responds to the sounds the objects make.
- Likes to visually follow where objects s/he has thrown land on the floor.
- Likes to visually follow where objects s/he has pushed off a high chair (or elsewhere) land on the floor.

Between the time period from 13-16 months the young child tends to exhibit the following characteristics:

- Explores her/his environment by handling objects and

Working in an Infant-Toddler Program

viewing them from different angles.
- Likes to take objects in and out of a container (bucket) and manipulate them.
- Still explores her/his environment by tasting objects (begins to use this sense more in combination with other senses to take in information).

Between the time period from 17-20 months the young child tends to exhibit the following characteristics:
- Eats with a spoon without assistance (very little smearing).
- Likes to take objects in and out of a container (small box) and manipulate them.
- Enjoys experimenting with different sounds made by toys (such as striking toys with various objects to produce sounds).

Between the time period from 21-24 months the young child tends to exhibit the following characteristics:
- Enjoys taking objects or toys apart to see what is inside.
- Can use all of her/his senses (taste, smell, touch, feel, see) to explore the environment.

Between the time period from 25-36 months the young child tends to exhibit the following characteristics:
- Able to sort objects by shape (circle, square, triangle).
- Able to sort objects by color (yellow, red, blue).
- Able to sort objects by size (big, small; biggest, smallest).
- Able to differentiate between objects that are smooth and rough.

This, too, is a time period in which rapid growth is observed. It represents a time in which the young child actively explores by seeing, smelling, tasting, hearing, and touching objects in her/his environment and assigning meaning to the information taken in through the senses.

Motor and/or Physical Development

Between the time period from birth to four months the young child tends to exhibit the following characteristics:
- Holds head up while on her/his stomach.

- Holds head up while held in sitting position.
- Can grasp an object (toy) placed in her/his hand.
- Able to touch both hands (in front).
- Extends hands away from her/his body touching objects within reach.

Between the time period from 5-8 months the young child tends to exhibit the following characteristics:

- Able to remain in a sitting position alone (on the floor or crib).
- Remains in a sitting position (on a high chair).
- Can move a toy (object) from one hand to the other.
- Can balance herself/himself on "all fours."
- Uses feet to hit nearby dangling objects (toys).
- Uses hands (or fists) to hit nearby dangling objects (toys).

Between the time period from 9-12 months the young child tends to exhibit the following characteristics:

- Is able to stand with only a little assistance.
- Holds onto a chair or table while standing.
- Pulls herself/himself up to stand by a chair or table.
- Crawls on "all fours."
- Climbs on stairs.
- Climbs on furniture.
- Able to feed herself/himself small morsels of food.
- Attempts to eat with a spoon (smears more that s/he eats).

Between the time period from 13-16 months the young child tends to exhibit the following characteristics:

- Walks while holding on from one chair (or table) to another.
- Walks alone from one point in the room to another.
- Eats with a spoon without assistance (smears less).
- Drinks from a cup with assistance.

Between the time period from 17-20 months the young child tends to exhibit the following characteristics:

- Walks up steps while holding onto a person (adult).

Working in an Infant-Toddler Program 39

- Walks up steps while holding onto a handrail.
- Walks down steps while holding onto a person (adult).
- Walks down steps while holding onto a handrail.
- Eats with a spoon without assistance (very little smearing).
- Drinks from a cup without assistance (spilling).
- Makes marks on a paper with a crayon.

Between the time period from 21-24 months the young child tends to exhibit the following characteristics:

- Able to walk and not fall.
- Able to run and not fall.
- Walks up steps without assistance.
- Walks down steps without assistance.
- Uses a spoon without assistance (no smears).
- Drinks from a cup without assistance (usually does not spill on his clothing while drinking).

Between the time period from 25-36 months the young child tends to exhibit the following characteristics:

- Can walk on tiptoes.
- Throws a ball (3-5 feet).
- Rides tricycle (with pedals).
- Can stand on one foot (balanced for one second).
- Is able to jump on two feet.
- Able to use a spoon.
- Able to use a fork.
- Able to drink from a cup with one hand.
- Uses the toilet (with assistance).

From birth to age 36 months marked growth in motor development and physical development is noted. Children in this age range experience the most rapid physical growth than in any other period in their lives. It is a time period where the young child needs large areas (inside and outside the home, or center) to develop motorically and physically.

By the time the child has reached 36 months, s/he has a full set of teeth and enjoys the opportunity to eat using a spoon, fork and cup without assistance.

Those Instructional Activities in Which the Paraprofessional in an Infant-toddler Program May Be Asked to Perform Include the Following*

- Provide instruction to a parent on how to bathe an infant.
- Read a story to a small group of toddlers.
- Provide instruction to a toddler on how to put on her/his outer garment.
- Observe and record specific developmental characteristics of a child in order for the teacher to develop a lesson plan.
- Operate an overhead projector during a lesson presented to parents (by the teacher) on the theme, "Nutrition and the Healthy Development of Young Children."
- Operate a slide projector during a lesson presented to toddlers by the teacher on the subject, "Animals We Love."
- Provide instruction to a toddler on how to snap her/his outer garment.
- Instruct a toddler on the proper way to hold and use a spoon.
- Provide instruction to a toddler on how to hang up her/his outer garments.
- Provide instruction to a parent on how to properly diaper an infant.
- Hold the hand of a toddler as s/he learns to walk up and down steps.
- Provide instruction to a parent on how to feed a nursing bottle to an infant.
- Operate a filmstrip projector during a lesson presented to parents by the teacher on the theme "Affective Development of Infants and Toddlers."
- Provide instruction to a parent on how to maintain a safe and healthy crib for an infant.
- Operate a film projector during a lesson presented to parents by the teacher on the topic, "Prenatal Care."
- Provide instruction to a toddler on how to hold a crayon.
- Tell a story to a small group of toddlers.

---

*This is not an exhaustive listing.

- Instruct a toddler on the proper way to drink from a cup.
- Repeat the vocal sounds of an infant and notify the teacher as to any new sounds produced by the child.
- Provide instruction to a parent on how to make educational toys (that are safe) using household objects and materials.

Those Noninstructional Activities in Which the Paraprofessional in an Infant-toddler Program May Be Asked to Perform Include the Following

- Maintain a daily attendance record of infants and toddlers in the program.
- Check records to see which children need health forms.
- Distribute newsletters and related correspondence to parents.
- Operate a variety of duplicating equipment.
- Operate a motor vehicle (van, bus, car) owned by the center for transporting children and/or parents.
- Dress and undress a young child.
- Assist the teacher in the physical arrangement of cribs, tubs, chairs, and tables used in the center.
- Assist in the preparation of meals.
- File application forms and related information materials.
- Assist in maintaining clean and safe playthings.
- Assist the teacher in carrying out an inventory of educational materials (blocks, records, etc.).
- Feed an infant.
- Assist the teacher in carrying out necessary clerical chores at the center.
- Diaper a young child.
- Assist in maintaining clean and safe cribs.
- Bathe an infant.
- Assist the teacher in supervising toddlers during lunch.
- Assist the teacher in storing audiovisual equipment (film projectors, etc.).
- Assist the teacher in greeting parents and children as they enter and exit the center.
- Assist the teacher in carrying out an inventory of supplies (diapers, crib sheets, etc.).

Guidelines for the Paraprofessional Working with Infants and Toddlers

1. Paraprofessionals working with infants and toddlers in early childhood education programs should always keep in mind the importance of their efforts (along with others) in the development of young children. This is especially true with regard to the child's intellectual development. As already pointed out in Chapter 1, Dr. Benjamin S. Bloom concluded that by the age of four, 50 percent of intellectual development has already occurred.
2. Infants and toddlers are constantly learning information. They are taking in information while sitting on the floor looking at a picture in a book or while lying in a crib having a diaper changed. Paraprofessionals should always look for opportunities to reinforce concepts and information. If the young child repeatedly hears a particular children's song (while sitting on the floor, while crawling, while sitting on your lap, or while being diapered) s/he will in time eventually learn it.
3. Paraprofessionals should keep in mind that infants and toddlers do not all develop at the same rate, and that areas of development such as cognitive, affective, sensory, perceptual, motor, and physical development frequently overlap with another. It would be difficult to understand the affective development of a young child without taking into consideration the cognitive, motor, sensory, perceptual, and physical developmental characteristics as well. A brief developmental listing was provided in order to provide the paraprofessional with an overview of certain characteristics of development to look for along approximate age ranges. It should be used only as a guide.
4. Paraprofessionals should try to provide an enriched and stimulating environment for infants and toddlers. Young children should be exposed to a plentiful variety of colorful toys and objects.
5. Infants and toddlers thrive on hearing your voice, or feeling your touch and hug, or seeing you smile. While some youngsters seem to demand almost all of your time, there

Working in an Infant-Toddler Program

are others who demand little, if any, of your attention. The paraprofessional should note that the child who demands so little often needs more of your attention than the child who seems to demand much. T. H. Bell (1972) cautions busy mothers (the same can be applied to busy paraprofessionals that, "Often the inactive, good-natured, noncrying baby needs this environmental stimulation the most."

6. Young children need opportunities to develop self-help skills. These are things the child can do for herself/himself. For example, the youngster should be allowed to use a spoon during meals even though s/he is messy. No one ever said that learning was going to be quick and free from messes and spills.
7. Paraprofessionals should be careful to avoid wearing jewelry that may be potentially harmful to the infant. Earrings, broaches, or necklaces can be easily pulled off by the child without the paraprofessional even knowing it. In a matter of seconds an earring or decorataive pin could lodge in the throat of an infant, resulting in death.
8. Infants and toddlers need time to hold and manipulate toys and objects in their environment. That is how they learn. Therefore, the paraprofessional must be sure that the toys and objects the young child holds (often tastes and smells) are not harmful. Make sure that playthings:
    a. are free from sharp, jagged edges that could cut a child;
    b. are small enough for the child to hold, yet large enough so the child won't choke on or swallow;
    c. are free from loose screws, nails, or fasteners in which the young child may either get cut, choke, or swallow;
    d. are cleaned frequently; and
    e. are removed when broken.
9. Paraprofessionals should make sure that cribs:
    a. are checked daily for unsafe toys and objects;
    b. are free from ropes, yarns, or ribbon in which the child may possibly strangle;
    c. have bumper cushions that are securely in place;
    d. have fitted bedding in order to reduce the chances of a young child crawling under it and suffocating; and

      e. are cleaned frequently in order to maintain proper health standards.
10. Youngsters in cribs should be given ample opportunities to be held and to sit, crawl, and explore outside as well as inside the crib. When the young child tires of a toy, replace it with another colorful one.
11. When the infant babbles, repeat the sounds s/he makes. This in turn encourages the infant to continue babbling and imitating new sounds. The vocal sounds (in addition to crying) of an infant form the foundation for language and communication. The paraprofessional should try to take advantage of opportunities to repeat the sounds the infant makes and to take note if and when the child imitates new sounds that the paraprofessional initiated.
12. The paraprofessional must never leave the young child unattended while in a bathtub or on a dressing table. The best advice is to have all bathing items and dressing items available before you bathe and dress the child. Having everything ready before you start will reduce the possibility of leaving the youngster unattended to get a washcloth, diaper, or any other item.
13. One very important function of a paraprofessional is to observe and record specific developmental characteristics of infants and toddlers. Information noted by the paraprofessional for a given youngster is helpful for the teacher in developing daily lesson plans. Keep in mind that your efforts in observing and recording the developmental characteristics of young children is appreciated by the teacher as well as the parents of infants and toddlers. A sample checklist to assist paraprofessionals in observing and recording developmental characteristics of young children is represented in Appendix B (Chapter 7).

SUMMARY

A brief overview of three types of programs in which paraprofessionals work with infants and toddlers was presented. They included: (1) a center-based program; (2) a home-based program; and (3) a home- and center-based program. A description and an example of each of the above programs was provided.

Although developmental characteristics often develop with one another, and not all infants and toddlers develop at the same rate, a selected listing of cognitive, affective, sensory, perceptual, motor, and physical developmental characteristics of these youngsters was presented. This developmental listing was not intended to serve as an exhausive listing. Instead, it was to be used by the paraprofessional as a general guide.

Instructional activities as well as noninstructional activities in which paraprofessionals work with infants and toddlers were described. They too were provided as a guide.

Practical guidelines for paraprofessionals to follow when working with infants and toddlers were discussed.

APPENDIX A

Chapter Review

The following sample questions are designed to assist the paraprofessional in reviewing information presented in this chapter. The answer key is located at the end of this appendix. (*Note*: training supervisors may decide to add questions of their own, based on local needs).

Multiple-choice Questions

1. Which of the following are the type of service(s) provided by the child and family resource program?
    ( ) A. Early childhood education
    ( ) B. Parent involvement
    ( ) C. Health and family social services
    ( ) D. All the above are correct
2. One of the oldest infant care centers in the nation is:
    ( ) A. The Children's Center at Syracuse University
    ( ) B. Was founded in 1964
    ( ) C. Both A and B are correct
    ( ) D. Florida Home Visitor Program
3. The approximate age range in which the young child should be able to feed herself/himself small morsels or food is:
    ( ) A. Between birth to 2 months
    ( ) B. Between 9-12 months
    ( ) C. Between birth to 4 months
    ( ) D. All the above are correct
4. Which of the following refers to a self-help skill?
    ( ) A. Using a spoon at meals
    ( ) B. Drinking from a cup
    ( ) C. Both A and B are correct
    ( ) D. None of the above are correct
5. Which of the following is *not* true regarding the instructional activities of a paraprofessional in an infant-toddler program?
    ( ) A. Supervise all the teacher's lesson plans

Working in an Infant-Toddler Program   47

   ( ) B. Read a story to a toddler
   ( ) C. Instruct a parent on how to bathe an infant
   ( ) D. Instruct a toddler on the proper way to hold a spoon
6. Which of the following are types of programs in which a paraprofessional works with infants and toddlers?
   ( ) A. Home- and center-based program
   ( ) B. Home-based program
   ( ) C. Center-based program
   ( ) D. All the above are correct
7. With regard to cognitive development, between the time period from birth to four months, the young child tends to exhibit which of the following?
   ( ) A. Makes vocal sounds
   ( ) B. Able to point to her/his own body parts
   ( ) C. Speaks in sentences
   ( ) D. All the above are correct
8. With regard to motor and/or physical development, between the time period from birth to four months, the young child tends to exhibit which of the following?
   ( ) A. Drinks from a cup without assistance
   ( ) B. Walks up steps
   ( ) C. Eats with a spoon
   ( ) D. None of the above are correct
9. By the time the child has reached 36 months, s/he:
   ( ) A. Can use a spoon and fork without assistance
   ( ) B. Can drink from a cup without assistance
   ( ) C. Both A and B are correct
   ( ) D. None of the above are correct
10. Paraprofessionals should make sure that cribs are:
    ( ) A. Cleaned frequently
    ( ) B. Checked daily for unsafe toys and objects
    ( ) C. Free from ropes, yarn, or ribbon
    ( ) D. All the above are correct
11. Playthings for infants and toddlers should be:
    ( ) A. Small enough for the child to hold, yet large enough so the child will not choke on or swallow
    ( ) B. Tiny so they can hold them
    ( ) C. Fragile

( ) D. None of the above are correct
12. With regard to affective development, between the time period from 5-8 months, a young child tends to exhibit which of the following?
    ( ) A. Enjoys using the pronouns "I" or "Me"
    ( ) B. Enjoys playing "Peek-a-Boo"
    ( ) C. Both A and B are correct
    ( ) D. None of the above are correct
13. Which of the following represents noninstructional activities of a paraprofessional in an infant-toddler program?
    ( ) A. Operate duplicating equipment
    ( ) B. File application forms
    ( ) C. Diaper a young child
    ( ) D. All the above are correct
14. According to Dr. Benjamin S. Bloom, about 50 percent of intellectual development occurs by the time the child reaches the age of:
    ( ) A. 1
    ( ) B. 4
    ( ) C. 3
    ( ) D. 2
15. Paraprofessionals who bathe and dress young children should:
    ( ) A. Never leave the young child unattended
    ( ) B. Have all bathing items available ahead of time
    ( ) C. Have all dressing items available ahead of time
    ( ) D. All of the above are correct

True/False Questions

    T   F
1. ( ) ( ) Infants and toddlers should be exposed to a plentiful variety of colorful toys and objects.
2. ( ) ( ) Observing and recording developmental characteristics of infants and toddlers is not a very important function of a paraprofessional.
3. ( ) ( ) Paraprofessionals are not allowed to feed infants.
4. ( ) ( ) By the time the child has reached 36 months,

Working in an Infant-Toddler Program

s/he generally has a full set of teeth.
5. ( ) ( ) The time span from birth to age 36 months witnesses a substantial growth period pertaining to the young child's affective development.
6. ( ) ( ) By the time the child reaches age eight months, s/he is able to say "da-da" or "ma-ma" but is not aware of the meaning.
7. ( ) ( ) The term "prenatal" refers to the time period after birth.
8. ( ) ( ) Center-based programs are those in which the young child is cared for at a given facility.
9. ( ) ( ) The child between 25-36 months can identify her/his full name.
10. ( ) ( ) According to the writer, a child playing *near* a child is the same as saying the child is playing *with* another child.
11. ( ) ( ) From birth to age 36 months marked growth in motor development and physical development is noted.
12. ( ) ( ) The infant or toddler who demands so little often needs more of your attention than the child who seems to demand much.
13. ( ) ( ) According to the writer, when the infant babbles, avoid repeating the sounds s/he makes.
14. ( ) ( ) Paraprofessionals should make sure that cribs have fitted bedding in order to reduce the chances of a youngster crawling under it and suffocating.
15. ( ) ( ) Men as well as women work in infant-toddler programs as paraprofessionals.

Answer Key

Answers to Multiple-choice Questions

1. D 5. A
2. C 6. D
3. B 7. A
4. C 8. D

9. C   13. D
10. D   14. B
11. A   15. D
12. B

Answers to True/False Questions

1. True   9. True
2. False   10. False
3. False   11. True
4. True   12. True
5. True   13. False
6. True   14. True
7. False   15. True
8. True

APPENDIX B

Suggested Readings and Films

Early Childhood Education

Arnstein, H. S. *The Roots of Love*. Indianapolis: Bobbs-Merrill, 1975.
Boegehold, B. D., Cuffaro, H. K., Hooks, W. S., and Klopf, G. J. (Eds.). *Education Before Five: A Handbook on Preschool Education*. New York: Bank Street College of Education, 1977.
Cratty, B. J. *Perceptual and Motor Development in Infants and Children*. New York: The Macmillan Company, 1970.
Evans, E. B., and Saia, G. E. *Day Care for Infants*. Boston: Beacon Press, 1972.
Gardner, D. B. *Development in Early Childhood*, 2nd ed. New York: Harper and Row Publishers, 1973.
Gordon, I. J. *The Infant Experience*. Columbus, Ohio: Charles E. Merrill Publishing Co., 1975.
Keister, M. E. *The Good Life for Infants and Toddlers*. Washington, D. C.: National Association for the Education of Young Children, 1973.
White, B. L. *Human Infants: Experience and Psychological Development*. Englewood Cliffs, New Jersey: Prentice-Hall, 1971.
Willis, A., and Ricciuti, H. *A Good Beginning for Babies: Guidelines for Group Care*. Washington, D. C.: National Association for the Education of Young Children, 1974.

Paraprofessionals

Costin, L. B. Training nonprofessionals for a child welfare service. *Children*, *13*:63-68, 1968.

Suggested Films

Film Title: "Mothers and Toddlers" (black and white)
Time: 22 minutes
Publisher: Martin Luther King, Jr. Family Center
Address: 124 North Hohne
Chicago, Illinois 69612

Film Title: "Infancy: Development of the Child Series" (color)
Time: 20 minutes
Publisher: CRM Film Productions

Address: 9263 Third Street
Beverly Hills, California 90210

Film Title: "Person to Person in Infancy" (black and white)
Time: 20 minutes
Publisher: Modern Talking Pictures
Address: 1212 Avenue of the Americas
New York, New York 10036

Film Title: "The Child: Part I, The First Two Months" (color)
Time: 29 minutes
Publisher: CRM Films
Address: 110 Fifteenth Street
Del Mar, California 92014

Film Title: "The Child: Part II, 2-14 months: (color)
Time: 28 minutes
Publisher: CRM Films
Address: 110 Fifteenth Street
Del Mar, California 92014

Film Title: "The Child: Part III, 12-24 months" (color)
Time: 29 minutes
Publisher: CRM Flims
Address: 110 Fifteenth Street
Del Mar, California 92014

Film Title: "Rock-A-Bye Baby" (color)
Time: 28 minutes
Publisher: Time-Life Films, Inc.
Address: 43 W. 16th Street
New York, New York 10011

Suggested Filmstrips

Filmstrip Series Title: "How An Average Child Behaves — From Birth to Age Five" (color, with records or cassettes)
Filmstrip 1: "From Birth to One: A Time of Remarkable Growth"
Filmstrip 2: "From One to Two: The Toddler

	Emerges"
Filmstrip 3:	"From Two to Three: Pushing for Independence"
Publisher:	Parent's Magazine Films, Inc.
Address:	52 Vanderbilt Avenue
	New York, New York 10017

REFERENCES

Arnstein, H. S. *The Roots of Love*. Indianapolis: Bobbs-Merrill, 1975.

Bell, T. H. *Your Child's Intellect: A Guide to Home-Based Preschool Education*. Salt Lake City: Olympus Publishing Co., 1972, p. 52.

Bloom, B. S. *Stability and Change in Human Characteristics*. New York: John Wiley and Sons, Inc., 1964.

Boegehold, B. D., Cuffaro, H. K., Hooks, W. S., and Klopf, G. J. (Eds.): *Education Before Five: A Handbook on Preschool Education*. New York: Bank Street College of Education, 1977.

Costin, L. B. Training nonprofessionals for a child welfare service. *Children*, *13*:63-68, 1968.

Cratty, B. J. *Perceptual and Motor Development in Infants and Children*. New York: The Macmillan Company, 1970.

Early Childhood and Family Development Programs Improve the Quality of Low-Income Families. Report to the Congress of the United States by the Comptroller General, Washington, D. C., February 6, 1979, p. 58.

Evans, E. B., and Saia, G. E. *Day Care for Infants*. Boston: Beacon Press, 1972, p. 10.

Gardner, D. B. *Development in Early Childhood*, 2nd ed. New York: Harper and Row Publishers, 1973.

Gordon, I. J. *The Infant Experience*. Columbus, Ohio: Charles E. Merrill Publishing Co., 1975, p. 115.

Hooks, W. S. Infant-toddler centers. In Boegehold, B. D., Cuffaro, H. K., Hooks, W. S., and Klopf, G. J. (Eds.): *Education Before Five: A Handbook on Preschool Education*. New York: Bank Street College of Education, 1977, pp. 103-107.

Keister, M. E. *The Good Life for Infants and Toddlers*. Washington, D. C.: National Association for The Education of Young Children, 1973.

Lazar, I., and Darlington, R. "Summary Report: Lasting Effects After Preschool." Washington, D. C.: U. S. Administration For Children Youth and Families (ACYF), 1979.

Stant, M. A. *The Young Child: His Activities and Materials*. Englewood Cliffs, New Jersey: Prentice-Hall, Inc., 1972, p. 7.

White, B. L. *Human Infants: Experience and Psychological Development*. Englewood Cliffs, New Jersey: Prentice-Hall, Inc., 1971.

Willis, A., and Ricciuti, H. *A Good Beginning for Babies: Guidelines for Group Care*. Washington, D. C.: National Association for The Education of Young Children, 1974.

CHAPTER 3

PARAPROFESSIONALS WORKING IN A DAY-CARE AND/OR PRESCHOOL PROGRAM

DESIRED LEARNER OUTCOMES

U PON completion of this chapter the paraprofessional will be able to:
- Define each of the following concepts and vocabulary words relative to early childhood education.
  day-care center program
  family group day-care
  fine differences
  gross differences
  home day-care
  in-home day-care
  laboratory/demonstration nursery school
  laboratory/demonstration preschool
- Identify and discuss the major types of programs in which a paraprofessional works with young children between the age of three and five years.
- List and discuss cognitive, affective, sensory, perceptual, motor, and physical development characteristics of young children between the age of three and five years.
- Identify instructional and noninstructional activities of a paraprofessional working in a day-care and/or preschool program serving children between the age of three and five years.
- Identify the major guidelines for paraprofessional to follow when working in a day-care and/or preschool program.

Prior to the mid-1960s, day-care programs and preschools in the United States generally offered play activities designed to enhance the affective development of young children, especially for those youngsters between the age of three and five years. In support of this observation J. E. Brophy, T. L. Good, and S. E. Nedler (1975) stated:

> Although day-care centers and nursery schools have existed for years, they became commonplace only in the 1960s with the advent of Project Head Start. Prior to that time, they were organized primarily as programs to provide play experiences to foster social and emotional development and were patronized primarily by middle- and upper-class families. However, with the establishment of Head Start centers and other preschools planned primarily for poor children, this emphasis on play and social-emotional development was often supplemented (in some extreme cases even supplanted) by an emphasis on stimulating the young child's intellectual development and preparing him for school.

The national concerns that surfaced during the mid-1960s, already discussed in Chapter 1, dramatically influenced the program emphasis of day-care and preschool programs. Early childhood programs were increasingly faced with the task of designing programs to meet the developmental needs of poor children as well as those of children from more affluent backgrounds. It was a time when early childhood programs, similar to those provided by Project Head Start, emerged. These programs were designed to offer educational opportunities to young children from low-income families, who might not be exposed to similar educational opportunities available to other young children from more affluent backgrounds.

More recently, early childhood programs have witnessed a growing interest in maintaining parental and family involvement as an important aspect of early childhood programs, especially for children from low-income families.

This chapter focuses on today's day-care and preschool programs that serve young children from age three to five years. Related programs serving infants and toddlers have already been presented in Chapter 2. Programs serving kindergarten-age children are discussed in Chapter 4.

For purposes of this book, day-care and preschool settings in which paraprofessionals work with young children (age 3-5 years) are defined as follows:

Types of Day-Care Settings

1. **DAY-CARE CENTER PROGRAM.** Also known as center-based day-care, this is a licensed child-care facility generally serving more than twelve young children. The actual number varies from state to state. A day-care center program is primarily an all-day early childhood program with a trained professional (teacher/head caregiver) and full-time and/or part-time paraprofessional personnel.
2. **FAMILY GROUP DAY-CARE.** This is child-care services generally provided in the renovated home of the caregiver. Renovations are based on licensing requirements. This type of program usually serves more than six children, yet not more than twelve children. The actual number varies from state to state. Some programs have a trained professional and a full-time and/or part-time paraprofessional.
3. **HOME DAY-CARE.** This is a licensed program in which child-care services are generally provided in the home of the caregiver, usually requiring only minor renovations. The term "family day-care" is often used interchangeably with "home day-care." In this type of setting, less than six young children are served. Again, the actual number may vary from state to state. Some programs have a trained professional who supervises a cluster of home day-care/family day-care programs, which are often staffed with full-time and/or part-time paraprofessionals.
4. **IN-HOME DAY-CARE.** No licensing is required here. It provides child care for one family. In this program, the caregiver either goes to the child's home or the child goes to the caregiver's home. It is rather rare to find trained professionals or trained paraprofessionals working in such a program.

Preschool-type Settings

1. **LABORATORY/DEMONSTRATION PRESCHOOL.** This term is used interchangeably with "laboratory/demonstration nursery school." This program is generally designed to provide training for teachers wanting to pursue a career in

teaching young children. Such programs are found on the campus of a two-year community college, college, or university.
2. **PRESCHOOL.** This is also referred to as a nursery school. A preschool program provides educational services for children ages three to five years. Their program usually has a separate half-day morning program for one group of preschoolers and a separate half-day of afternoon program for another group. Most preschools are privately owned. An increasing number of preschools are being sponsored by churches of various denominations.

Paraprofessionals who work in day-care or preschool programs usually receive some type of pre-service training and/or in-service training. For example, some paraprofessionals only receive one or two weeks of training prior to working with young children. Others may be pursuing a two-year associate of arts degree in early childhood education. Still others may be pursuing the bachelors degree and are serving as paraprofessionals (teacher interns) in a day-care or preschool program as part of their formal training (*see* Figure 1).

Whether the paraprofessional works in a day-care or preschool program, s/he must be knowledgeable of basic developmental characteristics of children ages three to five years. The following represents a selected listing of cognitive, affective, sensory, perceptual, motor, and physical developmental characteristics that are often observed in young children. It is not intended to serve as an exhaustive listing. Although developmental characteristics often overlap with one another, and not all children between the age of three and five years develop at the exact rate, as a group, they tend to exhibit the following characteristics along approximate age ranges.

Cognitive Development

The young child between the age of three and four years tends to exhibit the following characteristics:
- Can tell you the names and functions of more things in her/his environment.

Day-Care and/or Preschool Program

- Is rather talkative and enjoys telling you about exciting events in her/his life (real events).
- Is rather creative and enjoys telling you about exciting events in her/his life (make-believe events).
- Some are able to count to ten.
- Can memorize the words to several songs for children.
- Enjoys opportunities to "tinker" with things. Often likes to "fix" toys or objects.
- Can follow directions with one or two parts, such as "Give me the truck," or "Give me the truck and the paintbrush."

The young child between the age of four and five years tends to exhibit the following characteristics:

- Can sit and maintain interest in working at a given activity for a maximum of fifteen minutes in duration.
- Very eager to learn about new things in her/his environment. Is full of questions, such as "What is it?" or "How does it work?"
- Can tell you her/his age.
- Can follow directions with more than two parts, such as "Give me the crayon, the pencil, and the paper."
- Enjoys activities in which s/he is to find a solution independent of others, for example, "How many of these objects can you fit in this box?"

By the time the child has reached five years of age, more than 50 percent of intellectual development has already occurred. This is a time in development marked by the young child's highly inquisitive and uninhibited desire to explore almost everything in her/his environment and to find her/his own solutions to problems. Paraprofessionals working with this age group should try not to be easily upset when repeatedly asked "What is this for?" or "Why can't we do this?" The child uses these questions to learn about her/his environment and the world around her/him.

Affective Development

The young child between the age of three and four years tends to exhibit the following characteristics:

- Can tell you if she is a girl or he is a boy.
- Can tell you if another child is a boy or girl.
- Begins to respond in a more positive way to rules.
- Is more willing to share toys with other children, although s/he still often finds it difficult to do so.
- Is becoming more socially responsible and willing to say "please," or "thank you."
- Shows an increased interest in having personal contact with children, especially with those her/his own age. Sometimes a friendly "shove" is her/his way of making such a contact.

The young child between the age of four and five years tends to exhibit the following characteristics:

- Is aware of her/his racial identity (for example, knows that s/he is black).
- Is aware of the racial identity of other children.
- Enjoys playing with other children.
- Has established a "best pal."
- Is often more interested in spending time with other children rather than with adults.
- Is often concerned with the feelings of other children, for example, will put her/his arm around another child who is crying from an injury.
- Frequently enjoys working or playing with a group of children.

Children between the age of three and five years are increasingly becoming socially responsible individuals. Paraprofessionals working with this age group are often surprised by the child's rather sudden use of "thank you," or "please" and willingness to follow rules that are a part of the day-care or preschool program. This is also a period of time in which the youngster enjoys playing and working with a best friend, as well as a favorite group of children, often consisting of two or three members.

Sensory and/or Perceptual Development

The young child between the age of three and four years

tends to exhibit the following characteristics:
- Can identify and name more colors.
- Can sort objects by texture (rough, smooth).
- Can sort more objects by shape.
- Can sort more objects by color.
- Can sort more objects by size. (These objects have *gross* differences — another name for *large* differences.)
- Can identify more objects that are alike or different (by seeing, touching, hearing, tasting, and/or smelling).

The young child between the age of four and five years tends to exhibit the following characteristics:
- Can arrange objects by color and shade, such as the lightest color blue to the darkest color blue.
- Can sort more objects by shape.
- Can sort more objects by size. (These objects have *fine* differences — another name for *slight* differences.)
- Can sort more objects by texture.
- Can identify more objects in the environment that are alike or different.
- Can look at a picture of three familiar objects and tell you which object does not belong. (For example, a dog, cat, and crayon.)
- Can listen to a recording of three familiar sounds and tell you which sound does not belong. (For example, the sound of a piano, guitar, and siren.)

The sensory and/or perceptual development of young children ages three to five years has progressed rather rapidly, in addition to their cognitive and affective development. This is a period of time in which young children are increasingly able to use their senses to identify gross differences and fine differences as well as likenesses in objects in their environment.

Motor and/or Physical Development

The young child between the age of three and fours tends to exhibit the following characteristics:
- Can draw a line (although not always very straight).

- Attempts to copy a circle (however, often looks distorted).
- Is able to pour liquids (water) from a pitcher (jar) with some spilling.
- Can put on her/his own shoes (unable to lace or tie).
- Can build a block tower stacked to seven blocks high.
- Can undress herself/himself.
- Can walk on a large straight line (marked on the floor with tape).
- Enjoys putting together puzzles (with six or less pieces).
- Can do a forward roll.
- Can catch a large ball with both arms extended in front of her/him.

The young child between the age of four and five years tends to exhibit the following characteristics:

- Can copy a square.
- Able to make straight cuts with a scissor (children's scissor).
- Can put on her/his own shoes and lace them (unable to tie).
- Can build a block tower stacked to ten blocks high.
- Can propel herself/himself on a swing.
- Can dress and undress herself/himself.
- Can use a variety of playground equipment (slide, rings, jungle gym, swing).
- Can print first name (printing is a term used to describe manuscript writing).
- Enjoys putting together puzzles (with up to eight pieces).
- Can catch a large ball with elbows bent at her/his sides.
- Can throw a baseball approximately 15-18 feet (overhand throw).

By the time young children have reached the age of five they have developed the necessary self-help skills for feeding, dressing, undressing, toileting, and washing face and hands without assistance. It is a time when their motor and physical development provides them more play opportunities including games in which they can catch and throw balls. In addition, they are able to enjoy a greater variety of playground equipment.

Instructional Activities of a Paraprofessional Working in a Day-care and/or Preschool Program

- Instruct a parent on how to make an educational game, such as a matching card game made from paint color charts or magazine pictures.
- Listen to a child tell a story s/he has invented.
- Operate a film projector for a teacher making a presentation to parents entitled, "The Developmental Characteristics of Young Children."
- Work with a small group of children (two or three) painting at art easels.
- Assist a child learning to pour rice from a pitcher to another container.
- Assist a child learning to sort objects by color.
- Use a tape recorder with a child to teach which sound does not belong from a series of three familiar sounds recorded.
- Assist a child learning how to put together a puzzle.
- Assist a child learning to pour water from a pitcher to another container.
- Assist a child learning the words to a new children's song.
- Work with a child learning to catch a large ball.
- Work with a child learning how to climb the ladder on a slide.
- Assist a child attempting to perform a forward roll on an exercise mat.
- Operate a filmstrip projector and record player for a teacher presenting a lesson to the children on the topic, "Workers In Our Community."

Noninstructional Activities of a Paraprofessional Working in a Day-Care and/or Preschool Program

- Laminate teacher-made materials by covering them with clear, self-adhesive vinyl.
- Assist some children in buttoning or zipping their outer garments.
- Operate duplicating machines used in order to make class-

room worksheets.
- Mix paint for the teacher.
- Assist the teacher in the physical arrangement of chairs, tables, easels, bulletin boards, and materials.
- Assist some children in toileting.
- Inspect the playground for glass or other sharp objects and to see if the equipment is in safe-operating condition.
- Collate a three-page newsletter prepared by the teacher.
- Assist children in tying their shoes.
- Drive a day-care or preschool-owned van to and from a field trip.
- Prepare juice for snack time.
- Maintain a library used by parents.
- Store exercise mats.
- Assist the teacher in maintaining an inventory of equipment and materials.

Guidelines for the Paraprofessional Working with Young Children in a Day-care and/or A Preschool Program

1. Paraprofessionals should try to provide equal opportunities for girls and boys to play with toys and materials, as well as games that encourage motor development. Historically, the professional literature has often noted that with regard to gross motor skills, boys tended to do better than girls. Today, an increasing number of professionals are challenging these findings. They argue that historically our culture has often said, "Boys should play with certain toys," or "Girls should play certain games." Resultantly, boys often played with certain toys and materials and engaged in games that encouraged gross motor development, while girls were often discouraged from participating in similar activities. Therefore, more and more professionals are arguing that differences in gross motor development may be more related to adult expectations, rather than actual developmental differences between girls and boys. The point here is that girls and boys should have equal opportunities to play with toys, materials, and games provided by the day-care or preschool program, regardless of the child's

Day-Care and/or Preschool Program

sex.

2. Young children between the age of three and five years need to be provided with opportunities in which they can learn to wait for their turn. Therefore, paraprofessionals should assist the teacher in structuring learning actitivies, which encourages youngsters to wait their turn. Games should be provided in which the young child is encouraged to wait her/his turn when playing with a group of children. "Farmer in the Dell" is one such game.

3. Although children in this age group tend to enjoy games in which groups of children are involved, competition between children should be minimized, and avoided if at all possible. Although not all professionals are in universal agreement, some professionals strongly recommend that children below the age of eight years are too young to be involved in activities that stress competition. In keeping with the philosophy, it is better for the paraprofessional to say to the child, "Jane, you kicked the ball far," and avoid saying "Jane you kicked the ball farther than Tom."

4. Whenever working with children between the age of three and five years try to stress positive behavior. For example, "Thank you for putting the building blocks away," or "Thank you for remembering to sit quietly during storytelling time." Young children need to know that you (the adult) appreciate their efforts. The author realizes that with some youngsters it may be easier to note negative or inappropriate behaviors, rather than positive behaviors. However, emphasize whatever positive behaviors are exhibited by the child. This in turn may influence the child to continue exhibiting positive behaviors.

5. This chapter pointed out that children in this age group are increasingly able to respond in a more positive way to rules. Paraprofessionals should try to be positive rather than negative when stating rules for young children to follow. For example, here are two ways in which rules can be given. The first rule is stated in negative terms and is not recommended to be used with young children, the second rule is stated in positive terms and is recommended:

Not Recommended: "Don't ever run when you are holding

scissors."

Recommended: "Only walk when you are holding scissors."

6. Since children in this age group can follow directions with more than two parts, the paraprofessional must make sure that her/his directions are given in a clear, concise manner. This will assist the child in following directions.
7. Paraprofessionals should be aware that these youngsters are highly inquisitive and eager to learn, and they tend to ask many questions. This is how they learn. Therefore, try to understand that repeated questioning, from these children, is a normal developmental characteristic.
8. These youngsters need opportunities to practice such self-help skills as feeding, dressing, undressing, toileting, and washing face and hands without assistance. Although it generally takes more time for the child to complete these tasks by herself/himself, the paraprofessional should try to avoid doing certain tasks for the child. In other words, even if it takes longer for the child to complete a self-help activity (within a reasonable time period), it is better for the child to be given an opportunity to attempt these tasks and time to practice. Development of self-help skills are important to the child's educational program. Therefore, time spent in practicing these skills are necessary and important.
9. The paraprofessional is obligated to follow the instructional and noninstructional assignments of the teacher in charge. Although the paraprofessional may not always agree with the teacher's decisions, the day-care and/or preschool program would probably function more smoothly if the teacher's instructions are followed.
10. Please note that all listings of instructional and noninstructional activities of paraprofessionals in day-care and preschool programs provided in this chapter are not intended to be exhaustive.

SUMMARY

Historically, prior to the 1960s, day-care and preschool programs generally provided play activities that focused on the affective development of youngsters between the age of three and five years. However, those national concerns that surfaced during the mid-1960s that dramatically influenced the program emphasis of day-care and preschool programs in the nation were cited. In particular, the attention given to the needs of poor children as well as those of children from more affluent backgrounds were discussed.

This chapter focused on day-care and preschool programs in which paraprofessionals work with young children between the age of three years and five years. Day-care settings included: (1) day-care center program; (2) family group day-care; (3) home day-care; and (4) in-home day-care.

Preschool settings included: (1) laboratory/demonstration preschool; and (2) nursery school/preschool.

Although developmental characteristics often overlap with one another, and not all children between the age of three years and five years develop at the same rate, a selected listing of cognitive, affective, sensory, perceptual, motor, and physical developmental characteristics of these youngsters were provided along approximate age ranges.

Representative instructional activities as well as noninstructional activities of paraprofessionals working in day-care and/or preschool programs for children between the age of three and five years were discussed.

Practical guidelines for paraprofessionals to follow when working in day-care and/or preschool programs were also presented.

APPENDIX A

Chapter Review

The following sample questions are designed to assist the paraprofessional in reviewing information presented in this chapter. The answer key is located at the end of this appendix. (*Note*: Training supervisors may decide to add questions of their own, based on local needs).

Multiple-choice Questions

1. Prior to the mid-1960s day-care programs and preschools in the United States:
   ( ) A. Generally offered play activities
   ( ) B. Served middle and upper-class families
   ( ) C. Centered on the affective development of young children
   ( ) D. All the above are correct
2. Which of the following pertains to family group day-care?
   ( ) A. Serves between 6-12 children
   ( ) B. Child care is provided in the renovated home of the caregiver
   ( ) C. Both A and B are correct
   ( ) D. Serves between 50-100 children
3. By the time the child has reached the age of five, s/he has developed which of the following self-help skills?
   ( ) A. Washing face and hands without assistance
   ( ) B. Uses the toilet without assistance
   ( ) C. Dresses and undresses without assistance
   ( ) D. All the above are correct
4. This chapter indicated that some professionals strongly argue that children below what age are too young to be involved in activities that stress competition?
   ( ) A. 8
   ( ) B. 10
   ( ) C. 11
   ( ) D. 9
5. According to the writer, home day-care:

( ) A. Serves less than 6 young children
( ) B. Is never provided in the home of the caregiver
( ) C. Serves more than 12 youngsters
( ) D. None of the above are correct

6. A laboratory/demonstration preschool may be found on the:
   ( ) A. Campus of a two-year community college
   ( ) B. Campus of a college
   ( ) C. Campus of a university
   ( ) D. All the above are correct

7. The term "preschool" is often used interchangeably with which of the following?
   ( ) A. Nursery school
   ( ) B. Day-care center
   ( ) C. Family group day-care
   ( ) D. In-home day-care

8. According to the writer, which of the following rules are recommended to be used with young children?
   ( ) A. "Don't run in the class."
   ( ) B. "Only walk in the class."
   ( ) C. "Avoid running in the class."
   ( ) D. All the above are correct

9. With the advent of Project Head Start, what were the following outcomes?
   ( ) A. Lower-class families were served
   ( ) B. Only upper-class families were served
   ( ) C. More emphasis was placed on intellectual development
   ( ) D. Both A and C are correct

10. The young child between the age of four and five years tends to exhibit which of the following?
    ( ) A. Is aware of her/his racial identity
    ( ) B. Is aware of the racial identity of the children
    ( ) C. Both A and B are correct
    ( ) D. None of the above are correct

11. According to the writer:
    ( ) A. Boys should only be allowed to play with certain toys and materials.
    ( ) B. Girls should only be allowed to play with certain

toys and materials
- ( ) C. Boy and girls should have equal opportunities to play with toys and materials
- ( ) D. None of the above are correct

12. Which of the following is another name for gross differences?
    - ( ) A. Large differences
    - ( ) B. Fine differences
    - ( ) C. Small differences
    - ( ) D. No differences

13. Which of the following represent instructional activities of paraprofessionals working in a day-care and/or preschool program?
    - ( ) A. Listen to a child tell a story
    - ( ) B. Assist a child learning to pour water from a pitcher to another container
    - ( ) C. Assist a child learning to perform a forward roll
    - ( ) D. All the above are correct

14. Which of the following is another name for fine differences?
    - ( ) A. Large differences
    - ( ) B. Small differences
    - ( ) C. Gross differences
    - ( ) D. All the above are correct

15. According to the writer, the young child between the age of four and five years can sit and maintain interest in working at a given activity for a maximum of how many minutes in duration?
    - ( ) A. 15
    - ( ) B. 30
    - ( ) C. 40
    - ( ) D. 60

True/False Questions

    T   F

1. ( ) ( ) Children between the age of three and five years are increasingly becoming socially responsible individuals.

Day-Care and/or Preschool Program

2. ( ) ( ) The writer points out that differences in gross motor development may be more related to adult expectations, rather than actual developmental differences between girls and boys.
3. ( ) ( ) It is important for the paraprofessional to inspect the playground for glass or other sharp objects and to see if the equipment is in safe-operating condition.
4. ( ) ( ) Project Head Start was designed primarily for children from upper-class families.
5. ( ) ( ) In-home day-care programs generally provides child care for one family.
6. ( ) ( ) The terms "laboratory/demonstration preschool" and "laboratory/demonstration nursery school" are used interchangeably.
7. ( ) ( ) Most in-home day-care programs have trained professionals and paraprofessionals.
8. ( ) ( ) Developmental characteristics of young children rarely overlap with one another.
9. ( ) ( ) By the time the child has reached five years of age more than 50 percent of intellectual development has already occurred.
10. ( ) ( ) The young child between the age of three and four years can tell you her/his sex.
11. ( ) ( ) The young child between the age of four and five has established a "best pal."
12. ( ) ( ) By the time the child reaches the age of three years, s/he should be able to copy a circle without any distortions.
13. ( ) ( ) By the time the child reaches the age of five, s/he can throw a baseball approximately 15-18 feet.
14. ( ) ( ) The majority of paraprofessionals working in day-care and preschool programs are women.
15. ( ) ( ) According to the writer, paraprofessionals should never be required to operate audiovisual equipment.

Answer Key

Answer to Multiple-choice Questions

1. D
2. C
3. D
4. A
5. A
6. D
7. A
8. B
9. D
10. C
11. C
12. A
13. D
14. B
15. A

Answers to True/False Questions

1. True
2. True
3. True
4. False
5. True
6. True
7. False
8. False
9. True
10. True
11. True
12. False
13. True
14. True
15. False

APPENDIX B

Suggested Readings and Films

Early Childhood Education

Fraiberg, S. *The Magic Years*. New York: Charles Scribner's Sons, 1959.
Hymes, J. L. *Early Childhood Education: An Introduction to the Profession*. Washington, D. C.: N.A.E.Y.C., 1968.
Hymes, J. L. *Teaching the Child Under Six*. Columbus, Ohio: Charles E. Merrill Publishing Co., 1968.
Liepmann, L. *Your Child's Sensory World*. New York: Dial Press, 1973.
Sprung, B. *Guide to Non-Sexist Early Childhood Education*. New York: Women's Action Alliance, 1974.
Stant, M. A. *The Young Child: His Activities and Materials*. Englewood Cliffs, New Jersey: Prentice-Hall, Inc., 1972.

Paraprofessionals

Gattman, E., and Hendricks, W. *The Other Teacher: Aides to Learning*. Belmont California: Wadsworth Publishing Company, Inc., 1973.
Highberger, R., and Schramm, C. *Child Development for Day Care Workers*. Boston: Houghton Mifflin Company, 1976.
Quill, J. *One Giant Step — A Guide for Head Start Aides*. Washington, D. C.: National Association for the Education of Young Children, 1968.

Suggested Films

Film Title: "Day Care Today" (color)
Time: 27 minutes
Publisher: Polymorph Films
Address: 331 Newbury Street
Boston, Massachusetts 02115

File Title: "Jenny is a Good Thing" (color)
Time: 20 minutes
Publisher: Modern Talking Pictures
Address: 1212 Avenue of the Americans
New York, New York 10036

Film Title: "My Art is Me" (color)
Time: 25 minutes
Publisher: University of California, Extension

Address: Media Center
Berkeley, California 94720

Film Title: "The Child: Part IV, Three-Year-Olds" (color)
Time: 28 minutes
Publisher: CRM Films
Address: 110 Fifteenth Street
Del Mar, California 92014

Film Title: "The Child: Part V, Four to Six-Year Olds" (color)
Time: 30 minutes
Publisher: CRM Films
Address: 110 Fifteenth Street
Del Mar, California 92014

Suggested Filmstrips

Filmstrip Series Title: "How An Average Child Behaves — From Birth to Age Five: (color, with records or cassettes)
    Filmstrip 4: "From Three to Four: Socialization is the Task"
    Filmstrip 5: "From Four to Five: Entering the Big World"
Publisher: Parent's Magazine Films, Inc.
Address: 52 Vanderbilt Avenue
New York, New York 10017

REFERENCES

Brophy, J. E., Good, T. L., and Nedler, S. E. *Teaching in the Preschool.* New York: Harper and Row Publishers, 1975, p. xi.

Fraiberg, S. *The Magic Years.* New York: Charles Scribner's Sons, 1959.

Gattman, E., and Hendricks, W. *The Other Teacher: Aides to Learning.* Belmont, California: Wadsworth Publishing Company, Inc., 1973.

Highberger, R., and Schramm, C. *Child Development for Day-Care Workers.* Boston: Houghton Mifflin Company, 1976.

Hymes, J. L. *Early Childhood Education: An Introduction to the Profession.* Washington, D. C.: N.A.E.Y.C., 1968.

Liepmann, L. *Your Child's Sensory World.* New York: Dial Press, 1973.

Quill, J. *One Giant Step — A Guide for Head Start Aides.* Washington, D. C.: National Association for the Education of Young Children, 1968.

Sprung, B. *Non-Sexist Education for Young Children: A Practical Guide.* New York: Women's Action Alliance, 1975.

Stant, M. A. *The Young Child: His Activities and Materials.* Englewood Cliffs, New Jersey: Prentice-Hall, Inc., 1972.

CHAPTER 4

PARAPROFESSIONALS WORKING IN A KINDERGARTEN PROGRAM

DESIRED LEARNER OUTCOMES

UPON completion of this chapter the paraprofessional will be able to:
- Define each of the following concepts, words, and names relative to early childhood education:
  Elizabeth Peabody
  frame-of-reference
  Friedrich Froebel
  kindergarten
  learning center
  Margarethe Meyer Schurz
  Susan E. Blow
  template
  William T. Harris
- Identify and discuss major events and individuals that have influenced the kindergarten movement.
- List and discuss cognitive, affective, sensory, perceptual, motor, and physical developmental characteristics of children in a kindergarten program.
- Identify instructional and noninstructional activities of a paraprofessional working in a kindergarten program.
- Identify major guidelines for a paraprofessional to follow when working in a kindergarten program.

This chapter deals with paraprofessionals working in a kindergarten program. Kindergarten refers to an early childhood education program for children between the age of five and six years on a regular basis for the one year, prior to entering the first grade. A considerable number of kindergarten programs are sponsored by the public school; some are operated as a component of a preschool or day-care program, while others are sponsored by churches, community groups, organizations, and/or agencies. Kindergarten programs, including those that are private and public, generally include a trained teacher and a staff of paraprofessionals. While some kindergarten programs may enroll four-year-old children, this chapter focuses on the paraprofessional working in a kindergarten program serving children between the ages of five and six.

A brief historical overview of the kindergarten movement reveals that Friedrich Froebel, an educator, holds the distinction of founding the first kindergarten. Froebel's kindergarten (children's garden) was established in Germany in 1837. Froebel's early childhood educational programs emphasized the need to educate young children in a garden atmosphere, surrounded by nature. According to D. H. Cohen and M. Rudolph (1977):

> ... Thus, Froebel's Kindergarten included the following elements: play, considered important for self-development; special games and songs, which served to enhance learning; construction with materials that had symbolic meaning as well as manipulative value; practice at various tasks, especially gardening, that served to build character; and nature study, which Froebel considered uplifting. An important component of the Froebelian Kindergarten was "creativity," which was assumed to occur through imitation followed by construction and production. Another component was active physical involvement with play materials.

The teaching of Froebel inspired one of his students, Margarethe Meyer (Mrs. Carl) Schurz, to develop a kindergarten of her own. In 1855, she founded the first kindergarten in the United States in her home in Watertown, Wisconsin. Schurz's kindergarten included her own children as well as those of relatives and friends. It is interesting to note that her kindergarten program was not conducted in English, but rather in German. In fact, many of the kindergartens that followed during this time period were conducted in German.

The first English-speaking kindergarten in the United States was founded by Elizabeth Peabody in 1860. Her privately owned kindergarten was located in Boston. Not long after opening her kindergarten, Elizabeth Peabody traveled to Germany to observe kindergarten programs in operation in order to obtain more training and information. Because of her efforts, she holds the distinction of being the pioneer for developing the kindergarten in America.

It wasn't until the early 1870s that the first public school kindergarten was established, which was part of a total school system program. The first public school kindergarten was founded by Susan E. Blow, along with the support of William T. Harris, in St. Louis, Missouri. William T. Harris was superintendent of schools and later became the U.S. Commissioner of Education.

In the years that followed, more and more kindergartens were established and new early childhood philosophies (often challenging Froebel's views) emerged. However, it was not until the mid-to-late 1950s and 1960s that interest in kindergarten, along with other early education programs, became such a national concern (*See* Chapter 1).

From the 1960s to the present time there has been an increased interest in kindergarten and other early childhood programs, with a focus on ways to better train kindergarten personnel, including paraprofessionals. In fact, the training of paraprofessionals working in early childhood programs, such as kindergarten programs, is a major trend today and will probably continue during the decade of the 1980s.

Paraprofessionals working in a kindergarten program (public or private) enter the field at any one of the levels represented in the Career Ladder Model (*See* Figure 1). Whether the paraprofessional works in a private or public kindergarten, there are certain developmental characteristics s/he must be knowledgeable about concerning children between the age of five and six years.

The following represents a selected listing of cognitive affective, sensory, perceptual, motor, and physical developmental characteristics that are often observed in young children. It is not intended to serve as an exhaustive listing. Although developmental characteristics often overlap with one another, and not all children between the age of five and six years develop at the exact rate, as a group, they tend to exhibit the following characteristics along approximate age ranges.

Cognitive Development

The child between the age of five and six years tends to exhibit the following characteristics:

- Is increasingly using information already learned in the past to solve present problems. (In other words, s/he applies and uses past information to deal with situations in the here and now.)
- Is able to sit and work at a given activity or task for a longer unit of time (approximately 20 minutes).
- Can tell you her/his first, middle, and last name.
- Can tell you her/his address, including street and state.
- Can tell you her/his telephone number.
- Can tell you the day and month of her/his birthday.
- Can count up to twenty.
- Is able to tell you that there are ten things and count them for you. (For example, can count up to 10 crayons.)
- Can tell you the days of the week.
- Can tell you the months of the year.
- Can tell you about an event that happened and relate it in the order in which it occurred. (For example, is able to tell you what happened first, second, and third.)
- Enjoys trying out newly learned words in sentences (sometimes invents words of her/his own).

This is a time in development in which the child is able to sit for longer periods of time and attend more carefully to important details in her/his work. Children in this age group need opportunities to experiment with various ways to solve problems in their environment and be able to talk about what they did first, second, and so forth, in order to apply and use past knowledge for solving problems.

Affective Development

The child between the age of five and six years tends to exhibit the following characteristics:

- Is often willing to please (especially adults who are signifi-

cant others).
- Enjoys playing with a group of children (2-4 members).
- Begins to realize that everyone has abilities — some similar and different from her/his own.
- Takes more responsibility for the proper care of her/his toys, clothes, and other personal items.
- Shows respect for the proper care of the toys, clothes, and personal items of others.
- Is becoming more aware that s/he has different emotions and is able to describe some of them. (For example, "I cry when I get a cut," or "I get scared when dad turns off the lights." They often like to act out their feelings during dramatic play.)
- Is increasingly aware of the different emotions exhibited by others. (For example, "Lisa hurt Frank's feelings.")
- Is expanding her/his frame-of-reference, another way of saying that the child is broadening her/his world by taking in new information from more experiences.

Although youngsters between the age of five and six years enjoy playing with a group of children, they also need opportunities to be alone and work out some of their ideas and feelings.

Another important aspect of development to take into consideration is that these youngsters are often very willing to please adults, especially those who are significant others. In a kindergarten classroom, a significant other could be the teacher as well as the paraprofessional.

Sensory and/or Perceptual Development

The child between the age of five and six years tends to exhibit the following characteristics:
- Can name more colors in her/his environment.
- Can match more colors.
- Can arrange more colors in terms of shade, such as lightest to darkest and in reverse order, darkest to lightest.
- Can name more shapes and find them in her/his environment.

Working in a Kindergarten Program   81

- Can arrange objects in terms of length, such as shortest to longest and in reverse order, longest to shortest.
- Can arrange objects in terms of weight, such as lightest to heaviest and in reverse order, heaviest to lightest.
- Can arrange objects in terms of height, such as shortest to tallest and in reverse order, tallest to shortest.
- Can identify a variety of foods by taste while blindfolded.
- Can identify a variety of odors, or fragrances, by smell while blindfolded.
- Can identify a variety of objects by touch while blindfolded.

The kindergarten classroom should be a place full of new and refreshing opportunities for youngsters to see, smell, hear, taste, and feel objects in their environment. It is a time where exciting "mystery boxes" can be filled with different items in which the child is asked to use different senses in order to identify these objects. Items can be added to the mystery box with finer differences, as the child's sensory and perceptual development increasingly matures.

Motor and/or Physical Development

The child between the age of five and six years tends to exhibit the following characteristics:

- Is able to draw more shapes, such as a triangle, rectangle, and others, with or without the aid of a template. (A template is a pattern or device that guides the child in tracing a shape. A template could be made of metal, plastic, wood, or cardboard.)
- Can use the toilet without assistance.
- Can print her/his full name (in manuscript letters).
- Can draw a picture of a person and include a head, body, legs, arms, and details.
- Can write the numerals: 0, 1, 2, 3, 4, 5.
- Can wash her/his face and hands without assistance.
- Can brush her/his own teeth without assistance.
- Can feed herself/himself, including using a butter knife, without assistance.

- Is able to lace and tie her/his own shoes.
- Can zip, lace, tie, and button her/his own clothes without assistance.
- Can march to music.
- Is able to skip and hop.
- Can put together puzzles with more pieces.

By the time the child reaches the age of five, her/his weight is generally five times greater than her/his birth weight. In addition, the child's height in relation to height at birth has now doubled.

Children between the age of five and six years are beginning to assume a more erect posture and are often characterized as getting "trimmer and taller." It is a time in which the child's motor development and physical development are enabling her/him to be a more independent individual.

Instructional Activities of a Paraprofessional Working in a Kindergarten Program

- Assist a child, following teacher directions, on the proper way to write a numeral.
- Read a story to a small group of children and then ask questions about the story.
- Assist a child in using a template to draw certain geometric shapes.
- Work with a child who is learning to count ten nails at the woodworking bench.
- Operate a cassette tape recorder for a child at a learning center in the classroom. (A learning center is an area set aside in the classroom for a particular activity.)
- Listen to a child tell you the day and month in which s/he was born.
- Observe and record the behaviors of young children to determine if they are able to lace and tie their own shoes.
- Operate a film projector, for the teacher, during a social studies lesson on the topic, "How Food Travels to the Supermarket."
- Assist a child, following teacher directions, on the proper way to print her/his name (in manuscript letters).

- Assist a child, following teacher directions, on the proper way to cut straight lines and curves with scissors.
- Observe and record the behaviors of young children to determine if they are able to zip, lace, tie, and button their own clothes.
- Listen to a child tell you the months of the year.

Noninstructional Activities of a Paraprofessional Working in a Kindergarten Program

- Assist the teacher in collecting familiar objects (items familiar to the child) that will later be used in mystery boxes for the child to identify.
- Assist the teacher in supervising children during field trips.
- Supervise young children on the school bus.
- Assist the teacher in storing wood for the woodworking center.
- Assist the teacher in cutting out pictures and letters for the classroom bulletin board.
- Assist the teacher in supervising young children during recess period.
- Collect milk money.
- Assist the teacher in mounting pictures painted by children during art.
- Operate a variety of duplicating equipment for the teacher.
- Assist the teacher in greeting children during arrival and dismissal.
- Assist the teacher by filing routine forms.
- Assist the teacher in arranging materials and equipment used for a learning center.
- Store and maintain art supplies and materials.
- Assist the teacher during cleanup time.

Guidelines for a Paraprofessional Working in a Kindergarten Program

1. As already noted, the paraprofessional working in a kinder-

garten is often viewed, by youngsters, as a significant other. The way in which you treat young children often influences the way in which they view themselves. If you treat a child with dignity and kindness, s/he in turn will tend to look at herself/himself as being a person of worth. However, if you treat her/him in a negative way, then it is possible for the child to develop a poor self-concept.
2. This is a period of time in the development of a young child in which s/he enjoys copying or imitating the action of adults, including the paraprofessional. Therefore, the paraprofessional should be aware that her/his behavior is often being observed by the young children in the program. This places a heavy responsibility on the paraprofessional to display healthy and mature behaviors while carrying out her/his responsibilities in the kindergarten. If the paraprofessional raises her/his voice when things do not go the way planned, then it is not surprising to observe youngsters copying or imitating similar behaviors. For example, during dramatic play a youngster may say, "I'll pretend that I'm Ms. Miller" and then proceed to raise her voice as if she were confronting some difficulty in the classroom.
3. Paraprofessionals should keep in mind that these youngsters often like to do things for themselves. For instance, a child tying her/his own shoes often takes longer to do it than if s/he had assistance. However, giving the child the opportunity to do it herself/himself is important for the child's development and, in particular, contributes to her/his feelings of independence.
4. Paraprofessionals should remember that although children in this age group tend to sit for longer periods of time (approximately 20 minutes), they still need large units of time for movement and the exploration of their environment. Sometimes a youngster will sit for a very long time just to please you, the adult. Paraprofessionals should not encourage children to do this.
5. When working with young children, be satisfied with small gains. Each gain, no matter how small, is an indication that growth is occurring.
6. Make sure that all materials are all ready before working on

an activity with a young child, especially when a group activity is involved. Having materials ready for use before starting will help to insure that the children's attention will be maintained during the activity.
7. Try to speak in a clear, concise manner. If a child does not understand a question, perhaps you can reword the question in simpler terms.
8. Find opportunities for the child to put into practice information already learned. For example, let her/him count ten blocks in the play center, ten nails in the woodworking center, ten shells in the science center, and so forth. This encourages the child to apply information learned to new situations.
9. Children in this age group are able to assume more responsibility for taking proper care of their toys, clothes, and personal items. In addition, they are learning to be responsible by showing respect for their property and the property of others. Paraprofessionals should give young children opportunities to be more responsible. This includes: allowing youngsters to hang up their own coats and garments; put away their own art projects and supplies; and to clean up their own work area after completing an activity.
10. These youngsters are eager to play and work with a group of children, usually consisting of two, three or even four individuals. Although five-year-olds enjoy interacting with other children, they also need opportunities to be alone and work out some of their own ideas and feelings. The paraprofessional should work closely with the teacher in order to structure a program that provides the necessary balance of group activities and individual activities for youngsters in this age range.

SUMMARY

This chapter provided a brief overview of the kindergarten movement, including the contributions of Friedrich Froebel, Elizabeth Peabody, Margarethe Meyer Schurz, Susan E. Blow, and William T. Harris.

Although some kindergarten programs enroll four-year-old

children, this chapter focused on the paraprofessional working in a kindergarten program serving young children between the age of five and six years.

A selected listing of cognitive, affective, sensory, perceptual, motor, and physical development characteristics of young children between the age of five and six years was presented.

Instructional and noninstructional activities of a paraprofessional, as well as guidelines for a paraprofessional to follow when working, were discussed.

APPENDIX A

Chapter Review

The following sample questions are designed to assist the paraprofessional in reviewing information presented in this chapter. The answer key is located at the end of this appendix. (*Note:* Training supervisors may decide to add questions of their own, based on local needs.)

Multiple-choice Questions

1. In which decade was it that the first public school kindergarten was established in the United States?
   - ( ) A. 1870s
   - ( ) B. 1860s
   - ( ) C. 1820s
   - ( ) D. 1840s
2. Which of the following is *not* correct regarding Margarethe Meyer Schurz's kindergarten?
   - ( ) A. It was founded in 1855
   - ( ) B. Was conducted in English
   - ( ) C. Privately owned
   - ( ) D. All the above are correct
3. Which of the following individuals have the distinction of founding the first public school kindergarten in the United States?
   - ( ) A. Susan E. Blow
   - ( ) B. William T. Harris
   - ( ) C. Both A and B are correct
   - ( ) D. Margarethe Meyer Schurz
4. The child between the age of five and six years tends to exhibit which of the following?
   - ( ) A. Can use the toilet without assistance
   - ( ) B. Can print her/his full name
   - ( ) C. Can draw a picture of a person and include a head, body, legs, arms, and details.
   - ( ) D. All the above are correct
5. By the age of five, approximately how many times does the

child's weight increase over their birth weight?
   ( ) A. Two
   ( ) B. Five
   ( ) C. Three
   ( ) D. Four
6. The first English-speaking kindergarten in the United States was founded by:
   ( ) A. Elizabeth Peabody
   ( ) B. Margarethe Meyer Schurz
   ( ) C. Susan E. Blow
   ( ) D. William T. Harris
7. By the age of five, approximately how many times does the child's height increase over their height at birth?
   ( ) A. Three
   ( ) B. Two
   ( ) C. Four
   ( ) D. Five
8. According to the writer, which of the following activities are recommended for encouraging young children to be more responsible individuals?
   ( ) A. Allowing the child to hang up her/his own clothes
   ( ) B. Allowing the child to put away her/his own work
   ( ) C. Allowing the child to clean up her/his own work area
   ( ) D. All the above are correct
9. The child between the age of five and six years tends to exhibit which of the following?
   ( ) A. Can zip, lace, tie, and button her/his own clothes
   ( ) B. Can brush her/his own teeth
   ( ) C. Both A and B are correct
   ( ) D. None of the above are correct
10. A template, used to assist a child in tracing shapes, can be made of:
    ( ) A. Metal
    ( ) B. Plastic
    ( ) C. Wood
    ( ) D. All the above are correct
11. Children between the age of five and six years:
    ( ) A. Assume a more erect posture

( ) B. Often characterized as getting "trimmer"
( ) C. Often characterized as getting "taller"
( ) D. All the above are correct
12. The first kindergarten in the United States was:
( ) A. Privately owned
( ) B. Sponsored by a school district
( ) C. Conducted in English
( ) D. All the above are correct
13. According to the writer, kindergarten programs are sponsored by which of the following?
( ) A. School districts
( ) B. Community groups, organizations, or agencies
( ) C. Private individuals
( ) D. All the above are correct
14. In a kindergarten classroom, a "significant other" could be:
( ) A. The teacher
( ) B. The paraprofessional
( ) C. Both A and B are correct
( ) D. None of the above are correct
15. The child between the age of five and six years tends to exhibit which of the following?
( ) A. Can tell you her/his first, middle, and last name
( ) B. Can tell you her/his address, including street and state
( ) C. Can tell you her/his home telephone number
( ) D. All the above are correct

True/False Questions

    T   F
1. ( ) ( ) Friedrich Froebel founded the first kindergarten.
2. ( ) ( ) The first public school kindergarten in the United States was founded in St. Louis, Missouri.
3. ( ) ( ) The term "expanding the child's frame-of-reference" is another way of saying that the child is broadening her/his world by taking in new information from more experiences.
4. ( ) ( ) By the time the child reaches age five, her/his

weight has generally increased ten times greater than her/his birth weight.
5. ( ) ( ) The first English-speaking kindergarten in the nation was located in Boston.
6. ( ) ( ) Developmental characteristics of young children tend to overlap with another.
7. ( ) ( ) The training of paraprofessionals working in early childhood programs is a major trend today.
8. ( ) ( ) Motor development concerns the degree to which the young child is able to effectively utilize large and small muscles.
9. ( ) ( ) Children between the age of five and six years are not capable of taking proper care of their toys, clothes, and personal items.
10. ( ) ( ) Children in the age group discussed in this chapter are increasingly eager to play and work with a group of children, usually consisting of two, three, or four individuals.
11. ( ) ( ) By the time the child reaches the age of five, her/his height in relation to height at birth has tripled.
12. ( ) ( ) According to the writer, the kindergarten classroom should be a place full of new and refreshing opportunities for youngsters to see, smell, hear, taste, and feel objects in their environment.
13. ( ) ( ) Although youngsters between the age of five and six years enjoy playing with a group of children, they also need opportunities to be alone and work out some of their ideas and feelings.
14. ( ) ( ) Because of her many efforts, Elizabeth Peabody holds the distinction of being the pioneer for developing the kindergarten in America.
15. ( ) ( ) Paraprofessionals should make sure that all materials are ready for use before starting an activity.

Answer Key

Answers to Multiple-choice Questions

1. A
2. B
3. C
4. D
5. B
6. A
7. B
8. D
9. C
10. D
11. D
12. A
13. D
14. C
15. D

Answers to True/False Questions

1. True
2. True
3. True
4. False
5. True
6. True
7. True
8. True
9. False
10. True
11. False
12. True
13. True
14. True
15. True

APPENDIX B

Suggested Readings and Films

Early Childhood Education

Hymes, J. L., Jr. *Early Childhood Education: An Introduction to the Profession.* Washington, D. C.: National Association for the Education of Young Children, 1975.
Kemble, E. Starting Off on the Right Foot: The Case for Putting Early Childhood Education into the Public Schools. Washington, D. C.: American Federation of Teachers, AFL-CIO, (no date given).
Leeb-Lundberg, K. Friedrich Froebel: a friend. *Childhood Education,* 53:302-306, 1977.
Rice, M. F., and Flatter, C. H. *Help Me Learn: A Handbook for Teaching Children from Birth to Third Grade.* Englewood Cliffs, New Jersey: Prentice-Hall, Inc., 1979.
Seaman, A. C. A child's creed of needs. *Young Children,* XXX:166-167, 1975.
Snyder, A. *Dauntless Women in Childhood Education 1856-1931.* Washington, D. C.: Association For Childhood Education International, 1972.
Young, B. B. Take a fresh look around your kindergarten room. *Young Children,* XXX:160-165, 1975.

Paraprofessionals

Brighton, H. *Handbook for Teacher Aides.* Midland, Michigan: Pendell Publishing Company, 1972.
Hayden, R., Murdoch, R., and Quick, C. Teacher aides improve attention span. *Elementary School Journal,* 70:43-47, 1969.
Paraprofessionals in the Schools: How New Careerists Bolster Education. Arlington, Virginia: National School Public Relations Association, 1972.
Todd, V. E., and Hunter, G. H. *The Aide in Early Childhood Education.* New York: Macmillan Publishing Company, Inc., 1973.

Suggested Films

Film Title: "Concept Development in Outdoor Play" (color)
Time: 17 minutes
Publisher: Campus Film Distributors Corporation
Address: 20 E. 46th Street
 New York, New York 10017

Film Title: "Outdoor Play ... A Motivating Force for Learning" (color)
Time: 17 minutes
Publisher: Campus Film Distributors Corp.
Address: 20 E. 46th Street
New York, New York 10017

Suggested Slides

Slide Series Title: "Early Childhood: A Training Program for Teachers, Aides, Parents, Volunteers, and Administrators (color, cassette)
Program 1: "A Classroom Planned for Learning"
Program 2: "Focus on Art"
Program 3: "Focus on Discipline"
Program 4: "Focus on Development"
Publisher: Childhood Resources, Inc.
Address: 4105 N. Fairfax Drive
Arlington, Virginia 22203

REFERENCES

Brighton, H. *Handbook for Teacher Aides*, Midland, Michigan: Pendell Publishing Company, 1972.

Cohen, D. H., and Rudolph, M. *Kindergarten and Early Schooling*. Englewood Cliffs: New Jersey, Prentice-Hall, Inc., 1977, p. 4.

Hayden, R., Murdoch, R., and Quick, C. "Teacher Aides Improve Attention Span." *Elementary School Journal*, 70:43-47, 1969.

Hymes, J. L., Jr. *Early Childhood Education: An Introduction to the Profession*. Washington, D. C.: National Association for the Education of Young Children, 1975.

Kemble, E. "Starting Off on the Right Foot: The Case for Putting Early Childhood Education into the Public Schools." Washington, D. C.: American Federation of Teachers, AFL-CIO, (no date given).

Leeb-Lundberg, K. Friedrich Froebel: a friend. *Childhood Education*, 53:302-306, 1977.

Paraprofessionals in the Schools: How New Careerists Bolster Education. Arlington, Virginia: National School Public Relations Association, 1972.

Rice, M. F. and Flatter, C. H. *Help Me Learn: A Handbook for Teaching Children from Birth to Third Grade*. Englewood Cliffs, New Jersey: Prentice-Hall, Inc., 1979.

Seaman, A. C. A child's creed of needs. *Young Children*, XXX:166-167, 1975.

Snyder, A. *Dauntless Women in Childhood Education 1856-1931*. Washington, D. C.: Association For Childhood Education International, 1972.

Todd, V. E., and Hunter, G. H. *The Aide in Early Childhood Education*. New York: Macmillan Publishing Company, Inc., 1973.

Young, B. B. Take a fresh look around your kindergarten room. *Young Children*, XXX:160-165, 1975.

CHAPTER 5

PARAPROFESSIONALS WORKING IN A FIRST-GRADE PROGRAM

DESIRED LEARNER OUTCOMES

UPON completion of this chapter the paraprofessional will be able to:
- Define each of the following concepts and vocabulary words relative to early childhood education.
  lowercase letters
  peer group
  "press-for-limits"
  primary grades
  uppercase letters
- Identify certain historical factors that have had an influence on first-grade programs in the nation.
- List and discuss cognitive, affective, sensory, perceptual, motor, and physical developmental characteristics of six-year-old children.
- Identify instructional and noninstructional activities of a paraprofessional working in a first-grade program.
- Identify major guidelines for a paraprofessional to follow when working in a first-grade program.

This chapter concerns paraprofessionals working in a first-grade program with children between the age of six and seven years. There are public as well as private first-grade programs, however, the majority of youngsters in the United States attend public school first-grade programs.

Historically, schools in the United States have used a variety of grade-level plans. The two most widely used plans have been: (a) first grade through eighth (elementary level), ninth grade through twelfth (high school level); and (b) first grade through sixth grade (elementary level), seventh grade through ninth grade (junior high level), and tenth grade through twelfth grade (senior high level). It has been reported by R. H.

Nixon and C. L. Nixon (1971) that other kinds of grade level combinations have been attempted, as well, and that:

> There is a trend toward implementation of the concept of primary school, middle school, and high school. The authors envision an overall plan for young children-nursery through primary — covering the six-year span, to include children from three years of age through approximately eight years of age, or what is usually called third grade.

The major events that occurred during the mid-to-late 1950s, and 1960s influenced early childhood programs, including preschool programs, day-care programs, kindergarten programs, and first-grade programs as well.

In particular, many professionals and others in the community argued that there was a need for schools to return to the "basics" (reading, writing, and arithmetic) in an attempt to deal with the problem of so many high school students who were unable to read or perform related skills. In addition, during that time period it was pointed out that, based on Dr. Benjamin Bloom's research, waiting to educate the young child at age six was too late. It is interesting to note that today the field of education is increasingly witnessing a renewed emphasis on returning back to the basics. In support of this observation, G. S. Morrison (1976) projected that: ". . . The 1950s saw a resurgence of basic education philosophy and it is likely that a renewed emphasis will occur during the latter half of the 1970s and first part of the 1980s."

The professional literature has rather consistently indicated the beneficial effects of utilizing paraprofessionals in the schools, including those in the primary grades (kindergarten through grade three). According to the National School Public Relations Association: "Studies show that aides are fulfilling the major purposes expected of them: increasing the learning achievement of students and freeing teachers to use diagnostic planning and decision-making skills. Some surveys indicate that although installing an aide program takes additional funds, the per-pupil instructional costs can be lowered by using paraprofessionals" (*Paraprofessionals in the schools: How New Careerists Bolster Education*, 1972.)

This publication also noted that the largest concentration of paraprofessionals are found in the early grades.

Today, trained paraprofessionals play a very important part in the first-grade program. In addition to providing the teacher with more time to give youngsters individual attention, the per-pupil instructional costs are often lowered when paraprofessionals are utilized.

Although men and women serve as paraprofessionals in the first-grade programs, the majority are comprised of women. Paraprofessionals working in a first-grade program (public or private) enter the field at any one of the levels found in the Career Ladder Model presented in Chapter 1 (*see* Figure 1). However, most of them appear to enter the field at the first level, referred to as the paraprofessional aide stage.

It is important for paraprofessionals working in a public or private first-grade program to be aware of certain developmental characteristics of youngsters between the age of six and seven years. Although developmental characteristics often overlap with one another, and not all youngsters develop at the same rate, as a group, youngsters between the age of six and seven years tend to exhibit the following characteristics. (Again, this is not an exhaustive listing).

Cognitive Development

The young child between the age of six and seven years tends to exhibit the following characteristics:

- Understands about ten times more words than s/he did at age two. (Now understands approximately 2,500 words.)
- Language skills are becoming more refined, and s/he is less prone to invent words of her/his own.
- Is able to sit and work at a given task for longer periods of time (approximately 25 minutes).
- Increased interest in learning about things and events outside her/his home. (This is a time when the child broadens her/his knowledge base.)
- Is beginning to read. (Formal reading instruction is generally provided in first grade, however, some youngsters may have been exposed to it at an earlier time.)
- Is more able to take information learned and apply it to

more situations.
- Is beginning to perform simple arithmetic functions (addition, subtraction).
- Can tell time by the hour and half hour.
- Enjoys opportunities to solve problems by experimenting with old and new methods.
- Is still very inquisitive and full of questions, which reflect the child's desire to learn.

The child between the age of six and seven years is still rapidly developing in the area of cognitive development; sometimes this rapid growth is exhibited in more subtle ways than in previous times.

It is important to note that although, traditionally, children begin formal reading in the first grade, some youngsters may have already had opportunities to begin formal reading prior to first grade, while others may be enrolled in schools that do not introduce formal reading until the second grade.

Affective Development

The young child between the age of six and seven years tends to exhibit the following characteristics:

- Becomes more aware of her/his cultural background and heritage.
- S/he is very much influenced by the values of others in the environment (brothers, sisters, parents, teachers, paraprofessionals).
- The child's social contacts have now expanded rather dramatically. S/he how has a greater number of social contacts with different children and adults outside the home. (For example, the child has developed more social contacts in the neighborhood, school, and community.)
- Although youngsters in this age group often look at adults as a model to follow, they are also influenced by the values of the members of "the gang" (another way of saying peer group or children their own age).
- Frequently six-year-olds are observed changing from one group activity to another in the classroom.

- Often characterized as wanting to be the best in the class and sometimes sets goals or standards too high to achieve.
- Sometimes is stubborn and set in her/his ways.
- Frequently wants to know what behaviors significant others (adults and peers) consider as being "good" or "bad."
- Although these youngsters enjoy group activities, they still need and look forward to times when they can work alone at a particular task or assignment.

Children between the age of six and seven years are being influenced by the values and behavior of models from two major sources. One source includes significant others or models in the home, such as parents, sisters, brothers, and other family members. The second source includes significant others or models outside the home, such as other children from school and community as well as teachers and paraprofessionals. It is a time in development when the young child sometimes experiences discomfort in trying to decide when to comply with the wishes of significant others in the home *or* those outside the home.

Sensory and/or Perceptual Development

The young child between the age of six and seven years tends to exhibit the following characteristics:
- Listening skills are becoming more refined. S/he is learning how to hear and perceive differences and likenesses in letters, numbers, and words and is increasingly applying this information when completing reading, writing, and/or arithmetic assignments.
- Visual skills are also becoming more refined. S/he is learning how to see and perceive differences and likenesses in letters, numbers, and words and is increasingly applying this information when performing reading, writing, and/or arithmetic assignments.
- Often enjoys opportunities to trace letters, numbers, and words with her/his fingers.
- Is generally more visually attentive to specific details in a

picture.
- Notes shapes within letters, numbers, and words. (For example, points to the triangle in the uppercase [capital letter] letter *A* or points to a circle in the lowercase [small letter] letter *a*.)
- Is able to match more objects in terms of shape, size, height, and weight (involving fine differences).
- Is able to identify more objects in terms of similar and different functions.
- Although many can identify left and right parts of the body ("Touch your left leg"), a considerable number still have problems in consistently identifying left and right parts of the body.

Children in this age group are utilizing their sensory and perceptual skills to assist them during formal instruction in reading, writing, and arithmetic. Their sensory and perceptual world often takes on new meaning as they become more and more proficient in applying this information to everyday learning situations. These youngsters are becoming increasingly proficient in noting rather fine differences in objects and things inside as well as outside their immediate home environment. Their sensory and perceptual world is expanding beyond the home and into the neighborhood and community-at-large.

Motor and/or Physical Development

The young child between the age of six and seven years tends to exhibit the following characteristics:
- The average 6-year-old girl or boy is about 3.5 feet tall.
- The average 6-year-old girl weighs approximately 47 pounds.
- The average 6-year-old boy weighs approximately 48 pounds.
- Has about two permanent teeth.
- Overall body proportions and physical appearance approximates that of an adult.
- Is more proficient in skipping.
- Is more proficient in jumping.

- Is writing more letters and numbers.
- Is more proficient in hopping.
- Is more proficient in climbing.

Although these children are now more proficient in hopping, skipping, jumping, running, and climbing, their overall rate of physical growth tends to slow down in comparison to previous years.

It is a time when physical development has slowed down and cognitive development is still increasing at a rather rapid rate. During this period of time, youngsters are often motivated and possess the mental ability to print. Yet, frequently, they have not developed the necessary fine muscles in order to properly write with a pencil. Please keep in mind that this has to do with the child's motor development and does not reflect the child's lack of cognitive ability.

Instructional Activities of a Paraprofessional Working in a First-grade Program

- Listen to a child read.
- Work with a child learning to add one column of numbers (without "carrying").
- Read a story to a child and then ask questions concerning specific story details
- Assist a child in learning to tell time by the hours and half hours.
- Operate a filmstrip projector and record player for the teacher during a science lesson on the topic, "How A Plant Grows From Seed."
- Listen to a story told by a young child.
- Observe and record the behaviors of young children to determine if they can tell the difference between a penny and a dime.
- Assist a child learning to subtract one column numbers (without "borrowing").
- Operate a slide projector and a tape recorder for the teacher during an art lesson on the topic, "Painting Without A Brush."
- Listen to a child tell how s/he would solve a riddle.

- Play the game "Simon Says" with a group of children.
- Operate a film projector for the teacher during a PTA meeting on the topic, "How The Six-Year-Old Learns."
- Assist a child learning to print letters (in manuscript).
- Observe and record the behavior of young children to determine if they can consistently identify left and right parts of the body.

Noninstructional Activities of a Paraprofessional Working in a First-grade Program

- Assist the teacher in typing a series of work sheets.
- Collect lunch and milk money.
- File children's work samples.
- Operate a variety of duplicating machines.
- Laminate teacher-made math and reading flash cards.
- Supervise children on the bus.
- Assist the teacher in maintaining an inventory of classroom instructional materials and equipment.
- Take attendance. (This is not the same as maintaining the classroom register. Please note that the classroom register is only to be maintained by the teacher.)
- Distribute written notices for children to take home.
- Supervise opening exercises (for example, The Pledge of Allegiance).
- Store and maintain physical education equipment.
- Assist the teacher in ordering classroom supplies.
- Supervise children in the hall.
- Assist the teacher during cleanup time.
- Store and maintain audiovisual equipment and materials.

Guidelines for a Paraprofessional to Follow When Working in a First-Grade Program

1. Paraprofessionals should keep in mind that the motor development of six-year-olds does not always keep pace with their cognitive development. It is not uncommon for a youngster to be highly motivated and possess the mental ability to write letters, numerals, or words, yet may not

have developed the fine muscles necessary in order to properly write with a pencil. Remember, this does not mean that the child lacks the cognitive ability to write, but rather s/he needs time for fine muscles to develop.
2. Children in this age group look at parents, teachers, or paraprofessionals as significant others in their lives; at the same time they look at brothers, sisters, and other children as significant others, too. Resultantly, these youngsters sometimes become frustrated in trying to decide on what values they are going to accept: adult values or peer values. Paraprofessionals should be aware of this developmental characteristic and be understanding of the child's needs.
3. Youngsters sometimes "press for limits" in order to determine how far they can go before you set limits on certain behaviors. As significant others, the paraprofessional must work together with the teacher in order to maintain fair and consistent classroom rules. Once youngsters know that you keep your word and follow through on what is said, they will be less prone to press for limits.
4. Paraprofessionals must remember that a considerable number of six-year-olds have problems in consistently identifying left and right parts of the body. This means that these youngsters need *overlearning* opportunities. Overlearning refers to the presentation of a concept by means of repeated review of the concept (in this case left and right parts of the body) in creative and varied ways. Overlearning a concept can be attained by providing game-like learning activities. For example, "Simon says raise your right hand over your head." Other games could also be played in order to reinforce the same concept in creative and varied ways.
5. Youngsters in this age group often enjoy exploring new and exciting ways to solve everyday problems. These youngsters tend to be inquisitive and are almost constantly questioning to find solutions to problems that they consider important. The paraprofessionals should try to be patient with the young child, whose eagerness to learn often results in an almost constant flow of questions.
6. Paraprofessionals should keep in mind that although these youngsters often enjoy group interaction, they also need

time alone to try out their own ideas. Time should be set aside for them to work independent of the teacher, paraprofessional, and other children.
7. The paraprofessional is responsible for carrying out the education instructions of the teacher in charge. For example, if the teacher's lesson plan specifies that a specific method is to be used in reading, then that is the method that is to be carried out. The reading method specified by the teacher is to be used, even though the paraprofessional may prefer to use a different method. Remember, although the paraprofessional may not agree with all the educational decisions made, the classroom will probably operate more smoothly if the teacher's educational instructions are carried out properly.
8. Paraprofessionals working with six-year-olds must try to encourage the child who is having problems with a new or difficult learning activity. It is important for the paraprofessional to let the child know that mistakes are common, especially when an individual is involved in a new or difficult learning situation. This is important to these youngsters, since the professional literature reveals that they sometimes set unrealistic goals or standards for themselves.
9. A paraprofessional should make sure that all instructional materials, equipment, and supplies are ready for use prior to working with the young child. Having necessary items ready before initiating an activity reduces the chances of unnecessary distractions that occur during instruction.
10. Be aware that not all six-year-olds develop at the same rate, and the developmental characteristics of these youngsters often overlap with one another. The listing of cognitive, affective, sensory, perceptual, motor, and physical developmental characteristics was only intended to serve as a guide.

SUMMARY

Although there are private as well as public first-grade programs serving children between the age of six and seven years, the majority of these youngsters in the nation attend public school first-grade programs.

It was pointed out that, historically, certain major events that occurred during the mid-to-late 1950s, and 1960s, influenced first-grade programs, as well as preschool programs, day-care programs, and kindergarten programs in the nation.

Although developmental characteristics often overlap with one another, and not all youngsters between the age of six and seven years develop at the same rate, a selected listing of cognitive, affective, sensory, perceptual, motor, and physical developmental characteristics of young children was presented. This listing was to be used as a guide and not intended to serve as an exhaustive listing.

Instructional and noninstructional activities of a paraprofessionals to follow when working with six-year-olds were provided.

APPENDIX A

Chapter Review

The following sample questions are designed to assist the paraprofessional in reviewing information presented in this chapter. The answer key is located at the end of this appendix. (*Note*: Training supervisors may decide to add questions of their own, based on local needs.)

Multiple-choice Questions

1. The majority of paraprofessionals working in a first-grade program enter the field at which of the following levels?
   ( ) A. Paraprofessional aide stage
   ( ) B. Paraprofessional assistant stage
   ( ) C. Paraprofessional associate stage
   ( ) D. Both B and C are correct
2. Significant others in the home may include which of the following?
   ( ) A. Mother
   ( ) B. Father
   ( ) C. Brother and sisters
   ( ) D. All the above are correct
3. Significant others outside the home may include which of the following?
   ( ) A. Teacher
   ( ) B. Paraprofessional
   ( ) C. Students
   ( ) D. All the above are correct
4. Approximately how many times more words does the young child between the age of six and seven years understand than s/he did at age two?
   ( ) A. Thirty
   ( ) B. Ten
   ( ) C. Twelve
   ( ) D. Twenty
5. The largest concentration of paraprofessionals are found in:

( ) A. The early grades
( ) B. The junior high school
( ) C. The senior high school
( ) D. None of the above are correct
6. What are the beneficial effects of utilizing paraprofessionals in the first grade?
( ) A. Per-pupil instructional costs are often lowered
( ) B. The teacher has more time to teach
( ) C. Students receive more individual attention
( ) D. All the above are correct
7. The majority of young children in the nation attend:
( ) A. Private first-grade programs
( ) B. Public school first grade
( ) C. Company-sponsored first grade
( ) D. Both A and C are correct
8. According to the writer, what is the approximate maximum minutes that the young child between the age of six and seven years is able to sit and work at a given task?
( ) A. 10
( ) B. 12
( ) C. 25
( ) D. 5
9. The young child between the age of six and seven years is generally able to tell time:
( ) A. By the hour
( ) B. By the half hour
( ) C. Both A and B are correct
( ) D. None of the above are correct
10. What is the average weight of a six-year-old girl (in pounds)?
( ) A. 47
( ) B. 57
( ) C. 60
( ) D. 40
11. What is the average weight of a six-year-old boy (in pounds)?
( ) A. 48
( ) B. 40
( ) C. 57

( ) D. 60
12. What is the average height of a six-year-old girl or boy (in feet)?
    ( ) A. 2
    ( ) B. 3.5
    ( ) C. 2.5
    ( ) D. 4.5
13. Which of the following represent instructional activities of a paraprofessional working in a first grade?
    ( ) A. Observe and record the behaviors of young children
    ( ) B. Operate audiovisual equipment for the teacher
    ( ) C. Listen to a child read
    ( ) D. All the above are correct
14. Which of the following represent noninstructional activities of a paraprofessional working in a first grade class?
    ( ) A. Operate duplicating equipment
    ( ) B. File children's work samples
    ( ) C. Supervise children on the bus
    ( ) D. All the above are correct.
15. The term "basics," as used in this chapter, includes which of the following subjects?
    ( ) A. Arithmetic
    ( ) B. Reading
    ( ) C. Writing
    ( ) D. All the above are correct

True/False Questions

    T   F
1. ( ) ( ) According to the writer, six-year-olds understand only about 250 words.
2. ( ) ( ) The average six-year-old has about ten permanent teeth.
3. ( ) ( ) The overall rate of physical growth for six-year-olds tends to slow down in comparison to previous years.
4. ( ) ( ) The paraprofessional is responsible for main-

taining the official classroom register.

5. (　) (　) According to the writer, once youngsters know that you keep your word, and follow through on what is said, they will be less prone to "press-for-limits."
6. (　) (　) The paraprofessional is responsible for carrying out the educational instructions of the teacher in charge.
7. (　) (　) The motor development of six-year-olds does not always keep pace with their cognitive development.
8. (　) (　) The sensory and perceptual world of the six-year-old generally never expands beyond the home.
9. (　) (　) The overall body proportions and physical appearance of six-year-olds approximates that of an adult.
10. (　) (　) Six-year-olds sometimes experience discomfort in trying to decide when to comply with the wishes of significant others in the home as well as those outside the home.
11. (　) (　) The term "the gang" as used in this chapter, is another way of saying peer group.
12. (　) (　) Six-year-olds are less prone to invent words in comparison to previous years.
13. (　) (　) The primary grades include kindergarten through grade three.
14. (　) (　) Overlearning refers to the presentation of a concept by means of repeated review in creative and varied ways.
15. (　) (　) Six-year-olds rarely enjoy working with a group of children.

Answer Key

Answers to Multiple-choice Questions

1. A.
2. D
3. D
4. B

5. A
6. D
7. B
8. C
9. C
10. A

11. A
12. B
13. D
14. D
15. D

Answers to True/False Questions

1. False
2. False
3. True
4. False
5. True
6. True
7. True
8. False
9. True
10. True
11. True
12. True
13. True
14. True
15. False

APPENDIX B

Suggested Readings and Films

Early Childhood Education

Corbin, C. B. *A Textbook of Motor Development.* Dubuque, Iowa: William C. Brown and Company, 1973.
Cratty, B. J. *Perceptual and Motor Development In Infants and Children.* New York: Macmillan Publishing Company, 1970.
Lindberg, L., and Swedlow, R. *Early Childhood Education: A Guide for Observation and Participation.* Boston: Allyn and Bacon, Inc., 1976.
Margolin, E. *Young Children: Their Curriculum and Learning Processes.* New York: Macmillan Publishing Company, 1976.
Rice, M. F., and Flatter, C. H. *Help Me Learn: A Handbook for Teaching Children from Birth to Third Grade.* Englewood Cliffs, New Jersey: Prentice-Hall, Inc., 1979.
Seefeldt, C. *Social Studies for the Preschool-Primary Child.* Columbus, Ohio: Charles E. Merrill Publishing Company, 1977.

Paraprofessionals

Bowman, G. W., and Klopf, G. J. *New Careers and Roles in the American School.* New York: Bank Street College of Education for The Office of Economic Opportunity, 1968.
Brotherson, M. L., and Johnson, M. A. *Teacher Aide Handbook: A Guide for New Careers in Education.* Danville, Illinois: Interstate Printers and Publishers, 1971.
Clough, D. B., and Clough, B. M. *A Handbook of Effective Techniques for Teacher Aides.* Springfield, Illinois: Charles C Thomas, Publisher, 1978.
Hayden, R., Murdoch, R., and Quick, C. Teacher Aides Improve Attention Span. *Elementary School Journal, 70:*43-47, 1969.
Robb, M. H. *Teacher Assistants: A Blueprint for a Successful Volunteer-Aide Program.* Columbus, Ohio: Charles E. Merrill Publishing Company, 1969.
Wyckoff, L. M. School volunteers face the issues. *Phi Delta Kappan, 58:* 755-756, 1977.

Suggested Films

Film Title: "Foundations of Reading and Writing" (color)
Time: 40 minutes

Publisher: Campus Film Distributors Corporation
Address: 20 E. 46th Street
New York, New York 10017

Film Title: "Concept Development in Outdoor Play" (color)
Time: 17 minutes
Publisher: Campus Film Distributors Corporation
Address: 20 E. 46th Street
New York, New York 10017

REFERENCES

Bloom, B. S. *Stability and Change in Human Characteristics.* New York: John Wiley and Sons, Inc., 1964.

Bowman, G. W., and Klopf, G. J. *New Careers and Roles in the American School.* New York: Bank Street College of Education for The Office of Economic Opportunity, 1968.

Brotherson, M. L., and Johnson, M. A. *Teacher Aide Handbook: A Guide for New Careers in Education.* Danville, Illinois: Interstate Printers and Publishers, 1971.

Clough, D. B., and Clough, B. M. *A Handbook of Effective Techniques for Teacher Aides.* Springfield, Illinois: Charles C Thomas Publisher, 1978.

Corbin, C. B. *A Textbook of Motor Development.* Dubuque, Iowa: William C. Brown and Company, 1973.

Cratty, B. J. *Perceptual and Motor Development in Infants and Children.* New York: Macmillan Publishing Company, 1970.

Hayden, R., Murdoch, R., and Quick, C. Teacher aides improve attention span. *Elementary School Journal,* 70:43-47, 1969.

Lindberg, L., and Swedlow, R. *Early Childhood Education: A Guide for Observation and Participation.* Boston: Allyn and Bacon, Inc., 1976.

Margolin, E. *Young Children: Their Curriculum and Learning Process.* New York: Macmillan Publishing Company, 1976.

Morrison, G. S. *Early Childhood Education Today.* Columbus, Ohio: Charles E. Merrill Publishing Company, 1976, p. 13.

Nixon, R. H., and Nixon, C. L., *Introduction to Early Childhood Education.* New York: Random House, 1971, pp. 10-11.

Paraprofessionals in the Schools: How New Careerists Bolster Education. Arlington, Virginia: National School Public Relations Association, 1972, p. 48.

Rice, M. F., and Flatter, C. H. *Help Me Learn: A Handbook for Teaching Children from Birth to Third Grade.* Englewood Cliffs, New Jersey: Prentice-Hall, Inc., 1979.

Robb, M. H. *Teacher Assistants: A Blueprint for a Successful Volunteer-Aide Program.* Columbus, Ohio: Charles E. Merrill Publishing Company, 1969.

Seefeldt, C. *Social Studies for the Preschool-Primary Child.* Columbus, Ohio: Charles E. Merrill Publishing Company, 1977.

Wyckoff, L. M. School volunteers face the issues. *Phi Delta Kappan,* 58:755-756, 1977.

CHAPTER 6

PARAPROFESSIONALS WORKING IN A SECOND-GRADE PROGRAM

DESIRED LEARNER OUTCOMES

UPON completion of this chapter the paraprofessional will be able to:
- Define each of the following concepts and vocabulary words relative to early childhood education:
  auditory sequential memory
  listening comprehension
  massed practice
  reading comprehension
  spaced practice
  visual sequential memory
- Identify major factors that have influenced second-grade programs and the paraprofessional movement.
- List several benefits of utilizing paraprofessionals in the schools.
- List and discuss cognitive, affective, sensory, perceptual, motor, and physical developmental characteristics of seven-year-old children.
- Identify instructional and noninstructional activities in which a paraprofessional works with seven-year-old children.

This chapter deals with paraprofessionals working in a second-grade program (public or private) with youngsters between the age of seven and eight years.

Those major events that occurred during the mid-to-late 1950s, and 1960s (*see* Chapter 1), influenced early childhood programs, including second-grade programs, and the overall paraprofessional movement as well. This growing interest in utilizing paraprofessionals in early childhood education has emerged as a national priority in the field.

The professional literature reveals the beneficial effects of utilizing paraprofessionals in the second grade and at other grade levels in the schools of our nation. In fact, since the early 1960s there has been a steady increase in the amount of published professional books and articles regarding the topic of paraprofessionals. For example, H. G. Getz (1972) reported the following information: "The paraprofessional is a topic widely discussed in current professional literature; while only a few articles were seen in professional journals before 1959, a rather constant number was written from 1960-1964, and a mounting interest in paraprofessionals since 1966 has been reflected by the increasing number of articles and books available on the subject."

A nationally recognized study of fifteen major paraprofessional programs in the United States was carried out by Bank Street College of Education. The findings of this study, which was reported by G. W. Bowman and G. J. Klopf indicated the overall benefits of paraprofessionals in the schools. According to the study, paraprofessionals (the writers use the term "auxiliaries") are beneficial to many individuals in the following ways:

1. *For the pupil*, by providing more individual attention by concerned adults, more mobility in the classroom, and more opportunity for innovation;
2. *For the teacher*, by rendering his role more productive in terms of pupil outcome and more manageable in terms of teaching conditions;
3. *For the other professionals*, by increasing the scope and effectiveness of their activities;
4. *For the auxiliary*, by providing meaningful employment, which contributes to her own development and to the needs of society;
5. *For the school administrator*, by providing some solution — not necessarily the solution to his dilemma of increasing needs for school services, coupled with a shortage of professionals to meet these needs;
6. *For family life*, by giving auxiliaries (many of whom are or may someday be parents) the opportunity to learn child development principles in a real situation;
7. *For the community-at-large*, by providing a means through which unemployed and educationally disadvantaged persons may enter the mainstream of productivity

(1968).

Paraprofessionals working in a second-grade program enter the field at any one of the levels described in the Career Ladder Model as presented in Figure 1. The majority of paraprofessionals work in public schools. Although men work as paraprofessionals in second-grade levels, the largest percentage are comprised of women. It is interesting to note that the largest percentage of paraprofessionals who work in second-grade programs generally enter at the paraprofessional aide level.

Paraprofessionals working in a second-grade program (public or private) should be knowledgeable of the cognitive, affective, sensory, perceptual, motor, and physical developmental characteristics of young children between the ages of seven and eight years. Although developmental characteristics often overlap with one another, and not all children develop at the same rate, as a group, youngsters between the age of seven and eight years tend to exhibit the following characteristics. (*Note*: This is not an exhaustive listing:)

Cognitive Development

The young child between the age of seven and eight years tends to exhibit the following characteristics:

- Is becoming interested in weighing the various objects in her/his environment.
- Is becoming interested in activities involving liquid measurement (quarts, liters).
- Is becoming interested in activities involving linear measurement (inches, centimeters).
- Enjoys opportunities to solve mathematical reasoning problems, which have particular meaning to her/him.
- Enjoys being actively involved in weighing, measuring, or counting rather than just being told information or facts.
- Is learning to add two column numbers involving "carrying." Some can add three column numbers involving "carrying."
- Is learning to subtract two column numbers involving "borrowing." Some can subtract three column numbers

involving "borrowing."
- Is learning to read a thermometer.
- Is able to read with more comprehension (another way of saying that the child is reading with more understanding and meaning).
- Is able to count to 100 (or above) by ones, twos, fives, and tens.
- Some children are beginning to learn one column multiplication problems without "carrying."

As already pointed out in Chapter 1, Dr. Benjamin Bloom's research indicated that by the time a youngster reaches age eight, approximately 80 percent of her/his intellectual development has already occurred. The child's rapid growth during this time period is characterized by an almost constant quest for knowledge. In addition to constantly asking questions about her/his environment, the child wants to be actively involved in the learning process; these youngsters want to find out for themselves. They generally are not satisfied with just being told about facts. They want to solve problems by experimenting and doing. For example, if they are experimenting with linear measurement, they want first-hand opportunities to measure tables, chairs, people, walls, cars, and almost everything else inside or outside their home or school.

Affective Development

The young child between the age of seven and eight years tends to exhibit the following characteristics:
- Is more interested in team sports.
- Is more interested in social activities.
- Is becoming more competitive.
- Is becoming more aware of her/his own abilities, especially in comparison to those of their peer group.
- Is more able to wait her/his turn.
- Is often characterized as being courteous to others, including adults and peers. For example, s/he listens for a longer period of time without interrupting someone who is speaking.
- Enjoys "acting out" stories s/he has read, with particular

saying that the child's auditory sequential memory is becoming more refined. For example, hears three letters (K, M, A) and recalls the three letters in the same order they were heard (K, M, A).
- Is increasingly able to recall things that were seen in the exact order in which they were seen. This is another way of saying that the child's visual sequential memory is becoming more refined. For example, the child sees three numbers (9, 2, 8,) and recalls the exact order in which the numbers were seen (9, 2, 8).
- Is able to identify major body parts. Some still have problems identifying certain body parts, such as when told to "Point to your heel" or "Point to your wrists."
- Is able to identify left and right parts of the body ("Lift your right leg"), however, only a small number have problems in consistently identifying left and right body parts.

Youngsters in this age group are becoming quite skilled in adding meaning to information taken in from the senses. It is a time in development in which sensory and perceptual skills are becoming more and more refined, thus enabling the youngster to assign more meaning to things and events in her/his home, school, neighborhood, and community-at-large.

Motor and/or Physical Development

The young child between the age of seven and eight years tends to exhibit the following characteristics:
- Possesses the fine muscles development necessary in order to properly write with a pencil.
- Is more able to write words or short sentences copied from the chalkboard or a work sheet. Their manuscript writing is becoming more legible.
- By the age of eight years, s/he has approximately a total of ten or eleven permanent teeth.
- Possess the strength and physical development necessary in order to participate in a greater variety of physical education activities.
- Often motivated to practice a new motor task. In fact,

motor learning often improves (especially when learning a new skill) if the practice session includes *spaced* practice instead of *massed* practice. Spaced practice means that you provide the youngster with frequent practice sessions for short periods of time. Massed practice refers to a few practice sessions for long periods of time.
- Exhibits improved balancing skills.

Youngsters between the age of seven and eight years often experience increased strength, balance, and physical development. Resultantly, this improved motor ability broadens the child's opportunities for participation in sports and physical education activities. However, their growth in motor and physical development is not as rapid as the growth in cognitive development that occurs during this time.

Their improved fine muscle development assists them in properly writing (in manuscript) when using a pencil. This is in contrast to children between the age of six and seven years, who generally have not developed the fine muscles necessary in order to properly write with a pencil.

Instructional Activities in Which a Paraprofessional Works with Seven-year-old Children

- Correct student work sheets that do not require the subjective evaluation of the teacher.
- Assist a young child (following teacher instructions) to locate a book in the library.
- Operate an opaque projector for a small group of young children working on an art project taught by the teacher.
- Work with a child practicing a new motor skill during physical education period.
- Listen to a youngster read a story from her/his reading book.
- Assist a child measuring liquids.
- Listen to a child "act out" a story s/he has just read.
- Observe and record young children to determine how many are able to identify certain body parts, such as their elbows or heels.
- Assist a child in learning to read a thermometer.

- Read a story to a group of children and then ask a series of questions to see if they comprehended the specific information presented.
- Operate a record player during a music lesson, taught by the teacher on the topic "Music and Movement Exploration."
- Assist a young child working with math flash cards.
- Assist a youngster working on a science project for a classroom display.
- Operate a film projector during a social studies lesson taught by the teacher on the topic, "Getting Along With Others in the Community."
- Assist a youngster measuring a table.
- Assist a child (following teacher instructions) in completing an obstacle course involving movement exploration.

Noninstructional Activities in Which a Paraprofessional Works with Seven-year-old Children

- Assist the teacher in preparing student work sheets.
- Operate a variety of duplicating equipment.
- Assist the teacher in supervising young children during school assemblies.
- File completed work samples of the children in the class.
- Assist the teacher in arranging classroom chairs, desks, and tables.
- Assist the teachers in making reading and math flash cards.
- Assit the teacher in writing notices or assignments on the chalkboard.
- Assist the teacher in mounting students' art projects.
- Assist the teacher in collecting money from fund-raising project.
- Assist the teacher in supervising youngsters during field trips.
- Assist the teacher in preparing an inventory of classroom materials, equipment, and supplies.
- Assist the teacher during cleanup period.
- Assist the teacher in the preparation of a bulletin board

display
- Assist the teacher in the storing and maintenance of audio-visual equipment and materials.

Guidelines for a Paraprofessional to Follow When Working with Seven-year-old Children

1. Youngsters in the second-grade program need opportunities to observe properly formed manuscript writing. This is especially true of class work that includes manuscript writing appearing on the chalkboard, on work sheets, on notes, and on bulletin boards. It is important for teachers and paraprofessionals to make sure that writing they do in the classroom is the kind of manuscript writing that young children can use as a guide to follow.
2. The paraprofessional should remember to have all instructional materials and equipment ready for use before working with these young children. Unnecessary interruptions, which may be distracting to the child, could result if the paraprofessional had to stop an activity in order to get these necessary materials and equipment.
3. Research in the field reveals that overlearning by means of spaced practice sessions helps young children learn, especially when new motor tasks are presented. This means that paraprofessionals should work with the teacher in providing these youngsters with frequent practice sessions for short periods of time. It is important to note that overlearning opportunities can be provided in exciting and refreshing ways and not as a series of boring drills.
4. The paraprofessional needs to become aware of the things that children in this age group find of particular interest. The paraprofessional can be of considerable help to the teacher by sharing information regarding individual interests of children. This information helps the teacher in designing and carrying out a more personalized educational program. For example, if a certain child has a particular interest in collecting stamps, the teacher could personalize specific components of that child's educational program to include activities in which reference is made to this topic of

Working in a Second-Grade Program

interest. For instance, this youngster could be asked to add or subtract using stamp values during math or tell you how many more stamps are needed before a given page on her/his stamp album is completely filled. As already noted, children in the age group often tend to enjoy mathematic reasoning activities, which have particular meaning to them.

5. Youngsters in this age group need to be actively involved in the learning process. Paraprofessionals should keep in mind that the child's learning is enhanced when s/he is an active learner rather than an inactive learner. It is not enough to have the seven-year-old sit and just listen to a listing of facts. S/he needs to be actively involved by experimenting and trying out different ideas and procedures. This is how young children learn best.

6. Classroom rules for these youngsters should be stated in positive terms. Each rule should be stated in a clear, concise manner. In addition, paraprofessionals and teachers should be fair and consistent in maintaining rules in the classroom. Since seven-year-olds often exhibit an interest in rules, the paraprofessional and teacher should provide opportunities for these youngsters to be actively involved in generating classroom rules along with them.

7. The professional literature reveals that a child in this age range will often rush through a given activity and sometimes will stop working and become frustrated if her/his work does not meet her/his own high standards. Therefore, the paraprofessional should be aware of this characteristic and should alert the teacher when and if this behavior is being exhibited.

8. The paraprofessional should always check with the teacher whenever s/he is not sure as to what specific method or technique is to be used with a particular youngster. The teacher may have identified a particular method or technique s/he wants consistently used in order to enhance the child's learning.

9. This chapter revealed that youngsters in this age group are becoming more competitive and tend to enjoy team sports. However, it is not always easy for seven-year-olds (or some

adults for that matter) to lose a game or strike out at bat without "letting off steam." A paraprofessional should be aware of this characteristic and keep in mind that it is a part of normal development. However, if the child's emotions get out of hand, then the teacher or paraprofessional should intervene.

SUMMARY

It was reported that a review of the professional literature indicates that since the early 1960s there has been a steady increase in the amount of published books and articles concerning the topic of paraprofessionals in the schools.

The chapter focused on paraprofessionals working in a second-grade program with youngsters between the ages of seven and eight years.

A nationally recognized study of fifteen major paraprofessional programs, sponsored by Bank Street College, was cited. The overall findings of this study was presented, which revealed the multiple benefits of utilizing paraprofessionals in the schools.

A selected listing of cognitive, affective, sensory, perceptual, motor, and physical developmental characteristics of young children between the ages of seven and eight years was provided.

Instructional activities and noninstructional activities of a paraprofessional, as well as practical guidelines for a paraprofessional to follow when working on a second-grade program was discussed.

APPENDIX A

Chapter Review

The following sample questions are designed to assist the paraprofessional in reviewing information presented in this chapter. The answer key is located at the end of this appendix. (*Note*: Training supervisors may decide to add questions of their own, based on local needs).

Multiple-choice Questions

1. According to Dr. Benjamin S. Bloom's research, by what age does the youngster reach about 80 percent of her/his intellectual development?
    ( ) A. 8
    ( ) B. 4
    ( ) C. 2
    ( ) D. 3
2. Which of the following refers to auditory sequential memory?
    ( ) A. The ability to hear and see
    ( ) B. The ability to listen
    ( ) C. The ability to recall things in the exact order in which they are heard
    ( ) D. The ability to see with understanding
3. Which of the following refers to "spaced practice"?
    ( ) A. Few practice sessions for long periods of time.
    ( ) B. Frequent practice sessions for short periods of time.
    ( ) C. Few practice sessions
    ( ) D. Both A and C are correct
4. The seven-year-old tends to exhibit which of the following?
    ( ) A. Is rather opinionated
    ( ) B. Is quick to tell what s/he likes
    ( ) C. Is quick to tell what s/he dislikes
    ( ) D. All the above are correct
5. Which of the following is *not* correct, regarding paraprofessionals working in second-grade programs?
    ( ) A. Men work in second-grade programs

( ) B. The majority are comprised of men
( ) C. The majority work in public school programs
( ) D. Women work in second-grade programs

6. Which of the following refers to visual sequential memory?
   ( ) A. The ability to recall things seen in the exact order in which they were seen
   ( ) B. The ability to hear with understanding
   ( ) C. The ability to hear and see
   ( ) D. The ability to listen

7. The young child between the ages of seven and eight years tends to exhibit which of the following?
   ( ) A. Is becoming more competitive
   ( ) B. Is increasingly interested in social activities
   ( ) C. Is increasingly interested in team sports
   ( ) D. All the above are correct

8. Which of the following refers to "massed practice"?
   ( ) A. Few practice sessions for long periods of time
   ( ) B. Frequent practice sessions for short periods of time
   ( ) C. No practice at all
   ( ) D. None of the above are correct

9. The child who exhibits good listening comprehension skills is able to listen to information:
   ( ) A. Read to her/him with understanding
   ( ) B. Spoken to her/him with understanding
   ( ) C. Both A and B are correct
   ( ) D. None of the above are correct

10. Which of the following represents an instructional activity of a paraprofessional working in a second-grade program?
    ( ) A. Observe and record the behaviors of young children
    ( ) B. Assist a child measuring liquids
    ( ) C. Operate a film projector
    ( ) D. All the above are correct

11. Which of the following refers to reading comprehension?
    ( ) A. Reading with understanding
    ( ) B. Reading with meaning
    ( ) C. Both A and B are correct
    ( ) D. None of the above are correct

12. Which of the following represents a noninstructional ac-

tivity of a paraprofessional working in a second-grade program?
( ) A. Mounting art projects
( ) B. Assist the teacher during cleanup period
( ) C. File student's work samples
( ) D. All the above are correct

13. The child who hears three numbers (5,7,2) and recalls the three numbers in the exact order they were heard would be exhibiting:
( ) A. Auditory
( ) B. Auditory sequential memory
( ) C. Auditory and hearing
( ) D. Auditory and seeing

14. Since what decade has there been a steady increase in the amount of published professionals books and articles regarding the topic of paraprofessionals?
( ) A. 1960s
( ) B. 1900s
( ) C. 1910s
( ) D. 1920s

15. The seven-year-old tends to exhibit which of the following?
( ) A. Increased strength
( ) B. Increased balance
( ) C. Both A and B are correct
( ) D. None of the above are correct

True/False Questions

    T   F

1. ( ) ( ) Seven-year-olds need opportunities to observe properly formed manuscript writing so they can use it as a model.
2. ( ) ( ) Youngsters in the age group discussed in this chapter need to be actively involved in the learning process.
3. ( ) ( ) Classroom rules for seven-year-olds should be stated in negative terms.
4. ( ) ( ) Paraprofessionals are rarely asked to write on the chalkboard.

5. ( ) ( ) By the time the child reaches age eight, s/he has approximately a total of ten or eleven permanent teeth.
6. ( ) ( ) Only a small number of seven-year-olds have problems in consistently identifying left and right body parts.
7. ( ) ( ) Seven-year-olds are often characterized as being courteous to others, including adults and peers.
8. ( ) ( ) According to the writer, seven-year-olds tend to enjoy mathematical reasoning problems, which have particular meaning to them.
9. ( ) ( ) Developmental characteristics of seven-year-olds rarely overlap with one another.
10. ( ) ( ) The child between the age of seven and eight years tends to possess the fine muscle development that is necessary in order to properly write with a pencil.
11. ( ) ( ) With regard to seven-year-olds, their growth in motor and physical development is not as rapid as the growth in cognitive development that occurs during this time.
12. ( ) ( ) Research reveals that overlearning by means of spaced practice sessions helps young children learn, especially when new motor tasks are presented.
13. ( ) ( ) Seven-year-olds are often hard on themselves when evaluating the worth of their personal accomplishments.
14. ( ) ( ) The findings of the study by Bank Street College of Education, reported in this chapter, revealed that paraprofessionals are not very beneficial.
15. ( ) ( ) The utilization of trained paraprofessionals in early childhood education is a national priority in the field.

Answer Key

Answers to Multiple-choice Questions

1. A
2. C
3. B
4. D
5. B
6. A
7. D
8. A
9. C
10. D
11. C
12. D
13. B
14. A
15. C

Answers to True/False Questions

1. True
2. True
3. False
4. False
5. True
6. True
7. True
8. True
9. False
10. True
11. True
12. True
13. True
14. False
15. True

APPENDIX B

Suggested Readings and Films

Early Childhood Education

Blough, G. O., and Schwartz, J. *Elementary School Science and How to Teach it.* New York: Holt, Rinehart and Winston, 1974.
Copeland, R. M. *How Children Learn Mathematics.* New York: Macmillan Publishing Company, Inc., 1974.
Ford, B. E. The extended school day: privilege, not punishment. *Childhood Education,* 53:297-301, 1977.
Margolin, E. *Young Children: Their Curriculum and Learning Processes.* New York: Macmillan Publishing Company, Inc., 1976.
Nye, R. E., and Nye, V. T. *Music in the Elementary School.* Englewood Cliffs, New Jersey: Prentice-Hall, Inc., 1970.

Paraprofessionals

Beach, R. G. *Help in the School: Establishment of a Paraprofessional Program.* Philadelphia: Dorrance Company, 1973.
Bennett, W. S., Jr., and Falk, R. F. *New Careers and Urban Schools: A Sociological Study of Teacher Aide Roles.* New York: Holt, Rinehart and Winston, 1970.
Brighton, H. *Handbook for Teacher Aides.* Midland, Michigan: Pendell Publishing Company, 1972.
Gartner, A., Jackson, V., and Riessman, F. *Paraprofessionals Today.* Vol. 1. New York: Human Sciences Press, 1977.
Shank, P. C., and McElroy, W. *The Paraprofessionals or Teacher Aides: Selection, Preparation and Assignment.* Midland, Michigan: Pendell Publishing Company, 1970.
Timmons, J. A. Using paraprofessionals in the elementary school reading program. *Kappa Delta Pi Record,* 10:57, 1973.

Suggestsd Films

Film Title: "Dramatic Play...An Integrative Process For Learning" (color)
Time: 32 minutes
Publisher: Campus Film Distributors Corp.
Address: 20 E. 46th Street
New York, New York 10017

Film Title: "Foundations of Reading and Writing" (color)
Time: 40 minutes
Publisher: Campus Film Distributors Corp.
Address: 20 E. 46th Street
New York, New York 10017

REFERENCES

Beach, R. G. *Help in the School: Establishment of a Paraprofessional Program*. Philadelphia: Dorrance Company, 1973.

Bennett, W. S., Jr., and Falk, R. F. *New Careers and Urban Schools: A Sociological Study of Teacher Aide Roles*. New York: Holt, Rinehart and Winston, 1970.

Bloom, B. S. *Stability and Change in Human Characteristics*. New York: John Wiley and Sons, Inc., 1964.

Blough, G. O., and Schwartz, J. *Elementary School Science and How To Teach It*. New York: Holt, Rinehart and Winston, 1974.

Bowman, G. W., and Klopf, G. J. *New Careers and Roles in the American School*. New York: Bank Street College for the Office of Economic Opportunity, 1968, p. 9.

Brighton, H. *Handbook for Teacher Aides*. Midland, Michigan: Pendell Publishing Company, 1972.

Copeland, R. M. *How Children Learn Mathematics*. New York: Macmillan Publishing Company, Inc., 1974.

Ford, B. E. The extended school day: privilege, not punishment. *Childhood Education*, 53:297-301, 1977.

Gartner, A., Jackson V., and Riessman, F. *Paraprofessionals Today*. Vol. 1. New York: Human Sciences Press, 1977.

Getz, H. G. *Paraprofessionals in the English Department*. Urbana, Illinois: National Council of Teachers of English/Educational Resources Information Center, 1972, p. 8.

Hartley, R. E. and Goldenson, R. M. *The Complete Book of Children's Play*, rev. ed. New York: Thomas Y. Crowell Company, 1963, p. 199.

Margolin, E. *Young Children: Their Curriculum and Learning Processes*. New York: Macmillan Publishing Company, Inc., 1976.

Nye, R. E., and Nye, V. T. *Music in the Elementary School*. Englewood Cliffs, New Jersey: Prentice-Hall, Inc., 1970.

Rice, M. F., and Flatter, C. H. *Help Me Learn: A Handbook for Teaching Children from Birth to Third Grade*. Englewood Cliffs, New Jersey: Prentice-Hall, Inc., 1979, p. 13.

Shank, P. C., and McElroy, W. *The Paraprofessionals or Teacher Aides: Selection, Preparation and Assignment*. Midland, Michigan: Pendell Publishing Company, 1970.

Timmons, J. A. Using paraprofessionals in the elementary school reading program. *Kappa Delta Pi Record*, 10:57, 1973.

CHAPTER 7

PARAPROFESSIONALS WORKING IN A THIRD-GRADE PROGRAM

DESIRED LEARNER OUTCOMES

UPON completion of this chapter the paraprofessional will be able to:
- Define each of the following concepts and vocabulary words relative to early childhood education:
  kinesthetic cues
  cursive writing
  intersensory
  intrasensory
  tactile cues
  tactile-kinesthetic cues
- Identify certain historical factors that have had an influence on third-grade programs in the nation.
- List and discuss cognitive, affective, sensory, perceptual, motor, and physical developmental characteristics of eight-year-old children.
- Identify instructional and noninstructional activities in which a paraprofessional works with eight-year-old children.
- Identify the components of a sample morning and afternoon schedule for a paraprofessional working in a third-grade program.
- Identify major guidelines for a paraprofessional to follow when working with eight-year-old children.

The final chapter of this text focuses on paraprofessionals working in a third-grade program (public or private) for children between the ages of eight and nine years.

From a historical perspective, the major events that occurred during the mid-1950s and 1960s (*see* Chapter 1) have influenced early childhood programs, including third-grade programs, in the nation.

It has been previously noted that the professional literature has provided substantial support regarding the benefits of training paraprofessionals in the schools. In fact, the majority of paid and unpaid paraprofessionals are found in the third grade and other primary grades. In addition, the largest percentage of paraprofessionals in the early grades are comprised of women who generally enter the field at the paraprofessional aide stage. This is the first level of the Career Ladder Model represented in Figure 1.

Whether the paraprofessional works in a private or public third grade, there are certain developmental characteristics s/he must be knowledgeable about concerning young children between the ages of eight and nine years. The following represents a selected listing of cognitive, affective, sensory, perceptual, motor, and physical developmental characteristics that are often observed in young children. It is not intended to serve as an exhaustive listing. Although developmental characteristics often overlap with one another, and not all children between the age of eight and nine years develop at the same rate, as a group, they tend to exhibit the following characteristics along approximate age ranges.

Cognitive Development

The young child between the age of eight and nine years tends to exhibit the following characteristics:

- Is able to read and enjoy a variety of reading material, such as easy books, magazines, and comic books. Some can read newspapers.
- Enjoys communicating ideas and thoughts in written form. S/he likes to write party invitations, class notes, holiday greetings, club messages, letters, and other related forms of written communication.
- Is rather proficient in solving problems involving liquid measurement, and often enjoys opportunities to convert quarts to liters and other conversion combinations.
- Is able to add three (or more) column numbers involving "carrying."
- Is able to complete "math word problems," which involve reading, mathematical reasoning, and problem-solving

ability.
- Is able to subtract three (or more) column numbers involving "borrowing."
- Is able to complete two-column multiplication problems involving "carrying"; some can complete three columns (or more) multiplication problems.
- Is becoming more proficient in spelling.
- Some children are beginning to learn simple division problems.
- Is rather proficient in solving problems involving linear measurement and often enjoys opportunties to convert inches to centimeters and other conversion combinations.

During this age period, a rapid growth of intellectual development is observed. The research of Dr. Bloom has indicated that by the time the child reaches the age of eight, approximately 80 percent of intellectual development has already occurred.

The eight-year-old is a rather active learner and possesses a wide range of interest and cognitive skills, including the ability to read, write, spell, and complete a variety of mathematical operations (addition, subtraction, multiplication, and some can even divide.).

Affective Development

The young child between the age of eight and nine years tends to exhibit the following characteristics:
- Is very much concerned about what "the peer group" thinks about her/his wardrobe.
- Frequently is more concerned in looking good in the eyes of their peer group than in trying to please adults.
- Is often secretive about the rules and rituals of their peer group.
- Is rather opinionated and quick to let her/his feelings known.
- Is often more fascinated by the views of significant others outside the home than those inside the home.
- Is sometimes set in her/his ways and can be stubborn or

rebellious at times.
- Is very socially conscious and wants to be actively involved in planning classroom parties and other related social activities.
- Is as apt to make literal interpretations of classroom rules and regulations.

The young child in this age group tends to be fascinated by the views and wishes of significant others outside the home. These significant others include teachers, paraprofessionals, and especially members of her/his peer group. In fact "the peer group" often influences how s/he is to dress, talk, walk, act, and react to everyday life situations.

It is a time in development in which private clubs are founded; new club members are generally required to be initiated and follow a series of ceremonial rites. Once accepted, the club member is often sworn to secrecy and pledges her/his allegiance to the group.

Sensory and/or Perceptual Development

The young child between the age of eight and nine years tends to exhibit the following characteristics:
- Is able to consistently identify left and right body parts.
- Is able to make better use of visual information from her/his environment and assigns meaning.
- Is able to make better use of auditory information from her/his environment and assigns meaning.
- Relies less on the use of tactile-kinesthetic cues or information from her/his environment. (The term "tactile cues" pertains to information taken in by *touch*. "Kinesthetic cues" refers to information taken in through *muscle movement*. "Tactile-kinesthetic cues" refers to information jointly taken in through touch and muscle movement.)
- Is able to make better use of intersensory information. ("Intersensory" refers to two or more senses used in combination. The child uses the sense of sight in combination with another sense, perhaps the sense of hearing [or additional senses], and assigns meaning. An example would be

a child viewing a filmstrip [with audiotape].)
- Is able to consistently locate all body parts, including the wrist, heels, and elbow.

The sensory and perceptual development of the eight-year-old has progressed quite well. S/he is continuously making better use of intrasensory cues, (another way of saying taking in information from one sense at a time) as well as intersensory cues and assigning meaning.

Motor and/or Physical Development

The young child between the age of eight and nine years tends to exhibit the following characteristics:
- Is beginning to make the transition or change from manuscript writing (printing) to cursive writing. (Cursive writing involves writing with letters joined together.)
- Her/his height increases at a rate of approximately 5 percent a year.
- Is becoming skilled in throwing a ball.
- Is becoming skilled in catching a ball.
- Fine motor skills are continuously being refined.
- Her/his weight increases at a rate of approximately 10 per cent a year.
- Gross motor skills tend to be quite developed (running, hopping, jumping, skipping).
- Possesses the fine muscles necessary in order to hold and properly use a pencil, crayon, and/or paint brush for a longer period of time.

These youngsters are now ready to make the transition from manuscript writing to cursive writing. This newly acquired writing skill (motor skill) provides the child more opportunities to demonstrate her/his intellectual skills in communicating her/his ideas and thought in written form, including the composing of personal letters, class notes, club invitations and messages, party invitations and announcements, and many other kinds of written communication.

Although motor development has not developed as rapidly as intellectual development, s/he has systematically progressed and refined gross motor skills and fine motor skills, in that order respectively.

It is a time in which physical development has progressed but not as dramatically as intellectual development. During this time in development, height has increased at a rate of about 5 percent a year, and weight has increased at a rate of approximately 10 percent a year.

Instructional Activities in Which a Paraprofessional Works with Eight-year-old Children

- Assist a child, following teacher instructions, on the proper heading to use in writing a personal letter.
- Observe and record the behaviors of young children to determine if they are consistently able to identify left and right body parts.
- Listen to a child read a story from her/his reading book.
- Dictate a list of spelling words (taken from the child's reading book) to a young child.
- Operate a film projector for the teacher during a science lesson on the topic, "Solar Energy."
- Assist a child working on a math sheet in which the youngster is to convert quarts to liters and similar conversion problems
- Assist a child, following teacher instructions, on an assignment involving cursive writing.
- Assist a child working on a math work sheet in which the youngster is to add three-column numbers involving "carrying."
- Correct those completed written assignments of students that do not require the subjective evaluation of the teacher.
- Assist a small group of children working on a science project.
- Assist a child in locating a book from the library.
- Assist a child working on a math sheet in which the youngster is to convert inches to centimeters and similar conversion problems.
- Listen to a child read a short news article from a news-

paper and then ask her/him a series of questions about the story.

Noninstructional Activities in Which a Paraprofessional Works with Eight-year-old Children

- Assist the teacher in making classroom party decorations along with children.
- Assist the teacher in supervising young children during a field trip.
- File work sheets and other work samples of young children.
- Operate a variety of duplicating equipment.
- Assist the teacher during cleanup time.
- Assist the teacher in repairing children's books and workbooks.
- Distribute notices to children for them to take home.
- Assist the teacher in supervising children during lunch period.
- Assist the teacher in coordinating a fund-raising drive for a school project.
- Assist the teacher in designing a display for science projects completed by young children.
- Assist the teacher in supervising an after-school social function.
- Assist the teacher in maintaining an inventory in instructional materials and equipment.
- Assist the teacher in the physical arrangement of classroom desks, chairs, tables, and displays.
- Assist the teacher in completing clerical duties.

Guidelines for a Paraprofessional to Follow When Working with Eight-year-old Children

1. Paraprofessionals working with eight-year-old children must realize that these youngsters do not all develop at the same rate, and that cognitive, affective, sensory, perceptual, motor, and physical development frequently overlap with one another. Please remember that the developmental

listing included in this chapter and listings in previous chapters were provided to serve as a guide in assisting a paraprofessional working with young children. A sample morning schedule and afternoon schedule for paraprofessionals working in a third-grade program is represented in Figures 4 and 5, respectively.
2. Youngsters in this age group tend to be concerned about being actively involved in social functions. For example, if a party is being sponsored by the class, the teacher and paraprofessional should try to allow these youngsters to be actively involved in planning the event. Academics could also be introduced while these youngsters are assisting. For

Sample Morning Schedule For
A Paraprofessional Working
In A Third-Grade Program

9:00- 9:10	Collect lunch tickets Supervise opening exercises
9:10-9:40	Listen to Francis and Alonzo read from their reading book and then ask a series of comprehension questions.
9:40-10:10	Assist Tony, Roberta and Martha working on individual math worksheets.
10:10-10:30	Assist in supervising children during recess
10:30-10:50	Assist Lois and Fred in completing a cursive writing assignment
10:50-11:30	Duplicate worksheets for the teacher
11:30-11:40	Assist in clean-up
11:40	Assist in supervising children on their way to the lunchroom.

Figure 4. SAMPLE MORNING SCHEDULE.

Sample Afternoon Schedule For A Paraprofessional Working In A Third-Grade Program

12:20-12:45	Mix paints and get supplies ready for art period.
12:45- 1:15	File worksheets and other work samples completed by children.
1:15- 1:45	Duplicate, collate and staple a two-page parent newsletter
1:45- 2:15	Operate a film projector during a social studies lesson taught by the teacher
2:15- 2:45	Assist the teacher in preparing a classroom bulletin board display
2:45- 3:00	Assist the teacher in mounting art projects completed by children
3:00- 3:10	Assist in clean-up
3:10- 3:15	Distribute parent newsletters
3:15	Assist in supervising children on their way to the bus.

Figure 5. SAMPLE AFTERNOON SCHEDULE.

instance, children could be asked to write party invitations (in cursive writing) to teachers or parents. In addition, art, music, math, physical education, social studies, and other areas of curriculum could be incorporated as part of the overall party-planning experience.
3. The paraprofessional must keep in mind that these youngsters tend to be more concerned in pleasing their peer group than in pleasing adults. As an adult, try to realize that this is a normal characteristic of this age group and not necessarily a personal "attack" on the paraprofessional herself/ himself.
4. A paraprofessional working with eight-year-olds should try

to say what s/he means and to follow through on what is said in a firm yet gentle manner. This is especially important in that these youngsters are prone to make literal interpretations of classroom rules. The suggestion here is to only say what you are able to follow through on in a consistent and fair manner. In other words, only make statements or rules you can keep. In the long run, you will find that these youngsters will learn to respect you for being firm yet gentle in a fair and consistent way.

5. A paraprofessional working with eight-year-old children is often asked by the teacher to assist youngsters in learning activities that are designed to promote the child's comprehension. For example, if the youngster has just read a story in a book about three boys who went ice fishing, the following sample of structured questions to check comprehension, beginning with the easiest to the most difficult, may be used:

   A. Recall Question:
      1. What did you see in the picture?
   B. Clarification Questions:
      1. Who owned the fishing poles in the story?
      2. How many boys went fishing?
      3. Who owned the lake where the boys went fishing?
   C. Interpretation Questions:
      1. Why do you think the boys carried a tent?
      2. Why do you think the boys carried a heater?
   D. Probability Questions:
      1. What would have happened if the boys had not brought a tent?
      2. What would have happened if the boys had not brought a heater?
   E. Generalization Question:
      1. What did the boys in the story learn?

The same type of structured comprehension questions could be used if the paraprofessional was asked to check the child's listening comprehension. Using the previous story as an example, the paraprofessional would read the story to the child, and show the child any of the illustrations, and then ask structured questions beginning with the easiest to the most difficult. In the first example (reading comprehension), the child reads the story herself/himself and is then asked a series of comprehension questions by the paraprofessional. In the second example (listening comprehension), the paraprofessional reads the story to the child and asks her/him a series of structured comprehension questions.

6. A paraprofessional working with young children should avoid faking answers to questions in which s/he is not sure of the correct response. If you are not sure of the correct answer, be honest and say so. Perhaps you can suggest to the child to go to the library or to another specific source where the answer to the question could be obtained. It is not uncommon for eight-year-olds to test you to see if you are as good as your word. Keep in mind that the actions and reactions of paraprofessionals are often closely monitored or observed by these youngsters. A paraprofessional who is honest will probably find that in the long run s/he will probably earn their respect.

7. Make sure that all materials and equipment is ready for use before working with these youngsters. Failure to do so may result in distractions that may interfere with the child's learning.

8. The paraprofessional should be aware that the child's peers often exert a great deal of influence on how the eight-year-old dresses, talks, walks, acts, and reacts in the classroom in the school. As an adult, try to be understanding of the needs of youngsters going through this phase of development.

9. Children in the third-grade program need to be exposed to properly formed cursive writing. This means that paraprofessionals and teachers should make sure that any cursive writing that appears on the chalkboard, work sheets, or anywhere else in the classroom represents the type of cursive writing that these youngsters can use as a guide. Handwriting models (cursive writing) containing upper-case and lower-case letters of the alphabet are shown on next page.

Handwriting Models*

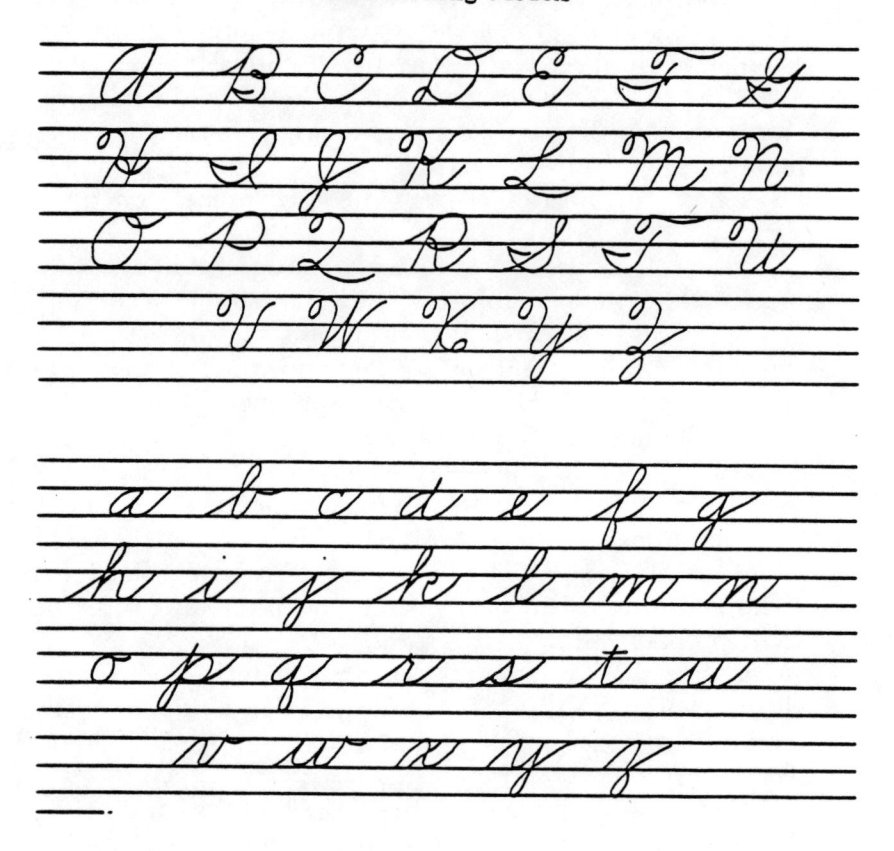

*Used with permission of the publisher, Zaner-Bloser, Inc., Columbus, Ohio. Copyright 1979.

10. This chapter pointed out that youngsters in this age group are often more concerned in pleasing the peer group than in trying to please adults; in addition, they are sometimes stubborn or rebellious. The important thing for the paraprofessional to remember is to avoid power struggles. For example, the young child may become frustrated in trying to decide whom to please: adults or peers? Resultantly, s/he may experience feelings of powerlessness or helplessness and make a bid for a sense of power or control by threatening the authority of those in charge, including the para-

professional or teacher, with such statements or acts as, "You can't make me," or "I won't do that," or encouraging other youngsters to act in the same manner. If such a situation should emerge, it is important for the paraprofessional to avoid getting locked into the child's game. When a power struggle erupts between a child and adult, nobody wins. Both come out of the experience feeling bad, and damage may be done to both the adult/child relationship and to the adult's position within the classroom as a whole. The paraprofessional needs to recognize a child's bid for power for what it is so that s/he does not become threatened. In this type of situation, an appropriate response from the paraprofessional might be, "No, Lee, I can't make you do it," then walk away. By acknowledging the bid for power and refusing to take part in the struggle, the impact of the situation is reduced, and Lee's game does not work. In most instances, Lee will go ahead and "do it."

SUMMARY

This chapter focused on paraprofessionals working in a third-grade program serving young children between the age of eight and and nine years.

It was reported that the majority of paid and unpaid paraprofessionals are found in the third grade and other primary grades in our nation's schools. Also, it was noted that the largest percentage of paraprofessionals in the early grades are comprised of women.

Although developmental characteristics often overlap with one another, and not all youngsters between the age of eight and nine years develop at the same rate, a selected listing of cognitive, affective, sensory, perceptual, motor, and physical developmental characteristics of these young children was provided.

Instructional activities as well as noninstructional activities of a paraprofessional working with young children between the age of eight and nine years were presented. A sample morning and afternoon schedule for a paraprofessional working in a third-grade program along with practical guidelines to follow was provided.

APPENDIX A

Chapter Review

The following sample questions are designed to assist the paraprofessional in reviewing information presented in this chapter. The answer key is located at the end of this appendix. (*Note*: Training supervisors may decide to add questions of their own, based on local needs.)

Multiple-choice Questions

1. The weight of an eight-year-old increases at a rate of approximately what percentage a year?
   ( ) A. 4
   ( ) B. 10
   ( ) C. 8
   ( ) D. 12
2. The height of an eight-year-old increases at a rate of approximately what percentage a year?
   ( ) A. 5
   ( ) B. 2
   ( ) C. 10
   ( ) D. 8
3. Which of the following are examples of intersensory information?
   ( ) A. Hearing, tasting, and seeing
   ( ) B. Seeing and feeling
   ( ) C. Tasting and hearing
   ( ) D. All the above are correct
4. The young child between the age of eight and nine years tends to exhibit which of the following?
   ( ) A. Tries to please peers more than adults
   ( ) B. Is rather secretive about the rules and rituals of "the gang"
   ( ) C. Is very social conscious
   ( ) D. All the above are true
5. The majority of paid and unpaid paraprofessionals are found in:

( ) A. The primary grades
( ) B. Third grade only
( ) C. Second grade only
( ) D. First grade only

6. Which of the following is an example of intrasensory information?
   ( ) A. Seeing and feeling
   ( ) B. Hearing
   ( ) C. Feeling, tasting, and seeing
   ( ) D. Smelling and tasting

7. In which of the following ways do peers influence the eight-year-old?
   ( ) A. How they dress and talk
   ( ) B. How they act and react
   ( ) C. Both A and B are correct
   ( ) D. None of the above are correct

8. Which of the following represents instructional activities of a paraprofessional working in a third-grade program?
   ( ) A. Assist a child in locating a book from the library
   ( ) B. Listen to a child read from a newspaper
   ( ) C. Both A and B are correct
   ( ) D. Operate duplicating equipment

9. Which of the following represents noninstructional activities of a paraprofessional working in a third-grade program?
   ( ) A. Dictate a list of spelling words to a young child
   ( ) B. Assist the teacher in maintaining an inventory of equipment
   ( ) C. Assist a child working on a cursive writing assignment
   ( ) D. Assist a child working on a math worksheet

10. According to the writer, cursive writing allows the child more opportunities to do which of the following?
    ( ) A. Write personal letters
    ( ) B. Write class notes
    ( ) C. Write party invitations and announcements
    ( ) D. All the above are correct

11. The term used interchangeably with "tactile" is:
    ( ) A. Touch

( ) B. Taste
( ) C. Smell
( ) D. Hear

12. The young child between the age of eight and nine years tends to exhibit which of the following?
    ( ) A. Is sometimes set in her/his ways
    ( ) B. Can be stubborn or rebellious at times
    ( ) C. Both A and B are correct
    ( ) D. None of the above are correct

13. According to Dr. Benjamin S. Bloom, by the time the child reaches the age of eight, approximately what percentage of intellectual development has already occurred?
    ( ) A. 80
    ( ) B. 20
    ( ) C. 10
    ( ) D. 45

14. The largest percentage of paraprofessionals in third-grade programs:
    ( ) A. Are comprised of men
    ( ) B. Are comprised of women
    ( ) C. Are comprised of individuals with bachelor's degrees
    ( ) D. Both A and C are correct

15. According to the writer, eight-year-olds tend to enjoy reading which of the following?
    ( ) A. Easy books
    ( ) B. Magazines
    ( ) C. Comic books
    ( ) D. All the above are correct

True/False Questions

T   F
1. ( ) ( ) The majority of paraprofessionals working in third-grade programs generally enter at the paraprofessional associate stage.
2. ( ) ( ) The eight-year-old is a rather active learner and tends to possess a wide range of interests.
3. ( ) ( ) These youngsters are often quick to let her/his feelings known.

Working in a Third-Grade Program   149

4. ( ) ( ) Tactile-kinesthetic cues refers to information jointly taken in through touch and muscle movement.
5. ( ) ( ) According to the writer, eight-year-olds are not ready to make the transition from manuscript to cursive writing.
6. ( ) ( ) The physical development of eight-year-olds has not progressed as dramatically as intellectual development.
7. ( ) ( ) Youngsters in this age group tend to be concerned about being actively involved in social functions.
8. ( ) ( ) Eight-year-olds tend to be more concerned in pleasing adults than in pleasing "the gang."
9. ( ) ( ) It is not uncommon for eight-year-olds to test you to see if you are as good as your word.
10. ( ) ( ) According to the writer, paraprofessionals should correct those completed written assignments of students that requires the subjective evaluation of the teacher.
11. ( ) ( ) Cursive writing involves writing with letters joined together.
12. ( ) ( ) Eight-year-olds tend to make literal interpretations of classroom rules.
13. ( ) ( ) Eight-year-olds are able to subtract three or more numbers involving "borrowing."
14. ( ) ( ) The developmental characteristics of eight-year-olds often overlap with one another.
15. ( ) ( ) Eight-year-olds are often more concerned with the views of significant others outside the home than with those inside the home.

Answer Key

Answers to Multiple-choice Questions

1. B   4. D
2. A   5. A
3. D   6. B

7. C
8. C
9. B
10. D
11. A

12. C
13. A
14. B
15. D

Answers to True/False Questions

1. False
2. True
3. True
4. True
5. False
6. True
7. True
8. False
9. True
10. False
11. True
12. True
13. True
14. True
15. True

APPENDIX B

Sample Checklist for Observing and Recording Developmental Characteristics

Child's Name: _____
Child's Age: _____

Description of Characteristic	Characteristic Observed			Date	Comments	Initials of the Paraprofessional
	Frequently	Sometimes	Never			

APPENDIX C

Suggested Readings and Films

Early Childhood Education

Corbin, C. B. *A Textbook of Motor Development.* Dubuque, Iowa: William C. Brown and Company, 1973.
Hutt, M. L., and Gibby, R. G. *The Child: Development and Adjustment.* Boston: Allyn and Bacon, Inc., 1962.
Margolin, E. *Young Children: Their Curriculum and Learning Processes.* New York: Macmillan Publishing Company, 1976.
Rice, M. F., and Flatter, C. H. *Help Me Learn: A Handbook for Teaching Children from Birth to Third Grade.* Englewood Cliffs, New Jersey: Prentice-Hall, Inc., 1979.

Paraprofessionals

Beach, R. G. *Help in the School: Establishment of a Paraprofessional Program.* Philadelphia: Dorrance Company, 1973.
Brighton, H. *Handbook for Teacher Aides.* Midland, Michigan: Pendell Publishing Company, 1972.
Brotherson, M. L., and Johnson, M. A. *Teacher Aide Handbook: A Guide for New Careers in Education.* Danville, Illinois: Interstate Printers and Publishers, 1971.
Clough, D. B., and Clough, B. M. *A Handbook of Effective Techniques for Teacher Aides.* Springfield, Illinois: Charles C Thomas Publisher, 1978.
Hale, J. M., and Ulmer, C. *Administrator's Guide to Training Paraprofessionals.* Englewood Cliffs, New Jersey: Prentice-Hall, Inc., 1972.
Paraprofessionals in the Schools: How New Careerists Bolster Education. Arlington, Virginia: Natural School Public Relations Association, 1972.

Suggested Filmstrips

Filmstrip Series Title: "The Art of Parenting" (color with cassettes)
    Filmstrip 1: "Communication"
    Filmstrip 2: "Assertion Training"
    Filmstrip 3: "Behavior Management: Motivation"
    Filmstrip 4: "Behavior Management: Methods"

Filmstrip 5: "Behavior Management: Discipline"
Publisher: Research Press Company
Address: 2612 N. Mattis Avenue
Champaign, Illinois 61820

REFERENCES

Beach, R. G. *Help in the School: Establishment of a Paraprofessional Program.* Philadelphia: Dorrance Company, 1973.

Bloom, B. S. *Stability and Change in Human Characteristics.* New York: John Wiley and Sons, Inc., 1964.

Brighton, H. *Handbook for Teacher Aides.* Midland, Michigan: Pendell Publishing Company, 1972.

Brotherson, M. L., and Johnson, M. A. *Teacher Aide Handbook: A Guide for New Careers in Education.* Danville, Illinois: Interstate Printers and Publisher, 1971.

Clough, D. B., and Clough, B. M. *A Handbook of Effective Techniques for Teacher Aides.* Springfield, Illinois: Charles C Thomas Publisher, 1978.

Corbin, C. B. *A Textbook of Motor Development.* Dubuque, Iowa: William C. Brown and Company, 1973.

Hale, J. M., and Ulmer, C. *Administrators Guide to Training Paraprofessionals.* Englewood Cliffs, New Jersey: Prentice-Hall, Inc., 1972.

Hutt, M. L., and Gibby, R. G. *The Child: Development and Adjustment.* Boston: Allyn and Bacon, Inc., 1962.

Margolin, E. *Young Children: Their Curriculum and Learning Processes.* New York: Macmillan Publishing Company, 1976.

Paraprofessionals in the Schools: How New Careerists Bolster Education. Arlington, Virginia: National School Public Relations Association, 1972.

Rice, M. F., and Flatter, C. H. *Help Me Learn: A Handbook for Teaching Children from Birth to Third Grade.* Englewood Cliffs, New Jersey: Prentice-Hall, Inc., 1979.

AFTERWORD

TODAY, the training of paraprofessionals to work with young children is a major trend in the field. This is a trend that will probably continue to remain in the forefront throughout the decade of the 1980s and well into the 1990s.

This text has attempted to provide the paraprofessional with a historical overview as well as a basic understanding of terminology, developmental characteristics, and guidelines in working with young children in a variety of settings. Also, it was intended to assist parents, teachers, and other professionals involved in the education and/or care of young children.

The author hopes that this volume has helped to explain rather complex research findings and information pertaining to early childhood education and development in clear, nontechnical terms. In addition, it is hoped that the reader enjoyed reading this book as much as the author enjoyed writing it.

GLOSSARY

AFFECTIVE DEVELOPMENT: The overall personal, emotional and social makeup of a young child.

AUDITORY SEQUENTIAL MEMORY: The ability to recall things heard in the exact order in which they were heard.

COGNITIVE DEVELOPMENT: The degree to which the young child is able to acquire ideas by effectively utilizing mental processes and thinking skills.

DAY-CARE: Primarily an all-day child-care program for young children. It provides child-care services five-days-a-week. The terms "day-care," "quality day-care," and "developmental day-care" are often used interchangeably.

FAMILY GROUP DAY-CARE: A licensed program in child care generally provided in the renovated home of the caregiver. This type of program usually serves more than six children, yet not more that twelve children.

HOME DAY-CARE: A licensed program in which child-care services are generally provided in the home of the caregiver, usually requiring only minor renovations. This type of program generally serves less than six young children.

IN-HOME DAY-CARE: No licensing is required. This type of program provides child care for one family. In this program, the caregiver either goes to the child's home or the child goes to the caregiver's home.

KINDERGARTEN: An early childhood education program for children, between the age of five and six years, attended on a regular basis for one year, prior to entering the first.

LABORATORY/DEMONSTRATION PRESCHOOL: A term used interchangeably with the term "laboratory/demonstration nursery school." This program is generally designed to provide training for teachers wanting to pursue a career in teaching young children. Such programs are found on the campus of a two-year community college, college, or university.

MASSED PRACTICE: This refers to few practice sessions for long periods of time.

MOTOR DEVELOPMENT: This concerns the degree to which the young child is able to effectively utilize large muscles and small muscles.

NIGHT-CARE PROGRAMS: The term "evening-care program" is often used interchangeably. A night-care program is designed to provide child care at a child-care center in the evening and/or during the entire night.

Paraprofessionals in Early Childhood Education: A person who helps the teacher in working with young children (infants to age 8) in a variety of activities sponsored by the program and is supervised by the teacher in charge.

Perceptual Development: This concerns the level at which the young child is able to assign meaning or understanding to information gained through the senses.

Physical Development: This refers to the young child's growth in terms of height, weight, posture, and related areas.

Preschool: This term is used interchangeably with the term "nursery school." A preschool program is basically designed to provide an educational program that primarily centers on the cognitive, affective, sensory, perceptual, motor and physical devleopment of young children. Preschools generally provide services 2-5 days a week, half a day each time.

Reading Comprehension: The ability to read with understanding

Sensory Development: This concerns the level at which the young child is able to effectively utilize her/his senses. This includes the sense of sight, hearing, taste, smell, and touch.

Spaced Practice: This refers to frequent practice sessions for short periods of time.

Special Child: A child who deviates from the "normal" in terms of cognitive, sensory, perceptual, motor, physical, or affective developmental characteristics to such a degree that s/he may need specialized materials, equipment, and/or services.

Visual Sequential Memory: The ability to recall things seen in the exact order in which they were seen.

AUTHOR INDEX

A

Almy, M., 26, 28
Arnstein, H. S., 51, 54

B

Beach, R. G., 130, 132, 152, 154
Bell, T. H., 43, 54
Bennett, W. S., Jr., 26, 28, 130, 132
Bloom, B. S., 10-11, 21, 23, 28, 42, 54, 96, 113, 117, 125, 132, 135, 154
Blough, G. O., 130, 132
Blow, S. E., 76, 78, 85, 87, 88
Boegehold, B. D., 51, 54
Bowman, G. W., 5, 6, 26, 28, 111, 113, 115-116, 132
Brandegee, A. S., 26, 28
Brighton, H., 92, 94, 130, 132, 152, 154
Brophy, J. E., 56, 75
Brotherson, M. L., 111, 113, 152, 154
Bruner, C., 26, 28

C

Clough, B. M., 111, 113, 152, 154
Clough, D. B., 111, 113, 152, 154
Cohen, D. H., 77, 94
Cohen, D. J., 26, 28
Copeland, R. M., 130, 132
Corbin, C. B., 111, 113, 152, 155
Costin, L. B., 51, 54
Cratty, B. J., 51, 54, 111, 113
Cuffaro, H. K., 51, 54

D

Darley, R. F., 26, 28
Darlington, R., 16-17, 23, 28, 54

E

Emmerling, F. C., 26, 28

Evans, E. B., 30, 51, 54

F

Falk, R. F., 26, 28, 130, 132
Flatter, C. H., 92, 94, 111, 113, 118, 132, 152, 154
Ford, B. E., 130, 132
Frailberg, S., 73, 75
Froebel, F., 76, 77, 85, 89, 92, 94

G

Gardner, D. B., 51, 54
Gartner, A., 130, 132
Gattman, E., 73, 75
Getz, H. G., 115, 132
Gibby, R. G., 152, 154
Goldenson, R. M., 118, 132
Good, T. L., 56, 75
Gordon, I. J., 31, 51, 54
Greer, J. V., 26, 28

H

Hale, J. M., 16, 28, 152, 154
Harris, W. T., 76, 78, 85, 87, 88
Hartley, R. E., 118, 132
Harvey, J., 18, 28
Hayden, R., 92, 94, 111, 113
Hendrick, J., 26, 28
Hendrick, W., 73, 75
Highberger, R., 73, 75
Hildebrand, V., 26, 28
Hooks, W. S., 30, 51, 54
Hunter, G. H., 26, 28, 92, 94
Hutt, M. L., 152, 154
Hymes, J. L., 73, 75, 92, 94

J

Jackson, V., 130, 132
Johnson, M. A., 111, 113, 152, 154,

Jordan, J. B., 26, 28

K

Kanawha, Z. C., 26, 28
Keister, M. E., 30, 51, 54
Kemble, E., 92, 94
Klopf, G. J., 5, 6, 26, 28, 54, 111, 113, 115-116, 132

L

Lazar, I., 16-17, 23, 28, 54
Leeb-Lundberg, K., 92, 94
Liepmann, L., 73, 75
Lindberg, L., 111, 113
Lombardo, V., 17, 26, 28

M

Margolin, E., 111, 113, 130, 152, 154
McElroy, W., 130, 132
Morrison, G. S., 10, 26, 28, 96, 113
Murdoch, R., 92, 94, 111, 113

N

Nedler, S. E., 56, 75
Nixon, C. L., 95-96, 113
Nixon, R. H., 95-96, 113
Nye, R. E., 130, 132
Nye, V. T., 130, 132

P

Peabody, E., 76, 77-78, 85, 88, 90

Q

Quick, C., 92, 94, 111, 113
Quill, J., 73, 75

R

Ricciuti, H., 51, 54
Rice, M. F., 92, 94, 111, 113, 118, 132, 152, 154
Riessman, F., 130, 132
Robb, M. H., 111, 113
Rudolph, M., 77, 94

S

Saia, G. E., 30, 51, 54
Schramm, C., 73, 75
Schurz, M. M., 76, 77, 85, 87, 88
Schwartz, J., 130, 132
Seaman, A. C., 92, 94
Seefeldt, C., 111, 113
Shank, P. C., 130, 132
Snyder, A., 92, 94
Sprung, B., 73, 75
Stant, M. A., 36, 54, 73, 75
Swedlow, R., 111, 113

T

Timmons, J. A., 130, 132
Todd, V. E., 26, 28, 92, 94

U

Ulmer, C., 16, 28, 152, 154

W

White, B. L., 51, 54
Willis, A., 51, 54
Wyckoff, L. M., 111, 113

Y

Young, B. B., 92, 94

SUBJECT INDEX

A

Affective Development
 Definition, 8, 157
Affective Development of children in
 Day-Care/Preschool Program, 59-60
 First-Grade Program, 98-99
 Infant-Toddler Program, 34-36
 Kindergarten Program, 79-80
 Second-Grade Program, 117-118
 Third-Grade Program, 135-136

B

Bay City Project, 11, 12

C

Certification of Paraprofessionals, 16
Child Care Volunteers, 4
Company-Sponsored Child Care, 13-16
Cognitive Development
 Definition, 8, 157
Cognitive Development of children in
 Day-Care/Preschool Program, 58-59
 First-Grade Program, 97-98
 Infant-Toddler Program, 32-34
 Kindergarten Program, 79
 Second-Grade Program, 116-117
 Third-Grade Program, 134-135

D

Day-Care Aides, 4
Day-Care Assistants, 4

E

Early Childhood Aides, 4
Early Childhood Auxiliaries, 4
Early Childhood Volunteers, 6
Early Education Aides, 6
Early Education Auxiliaries, 6

F

Ford Foundation, 11

G

Guidelines for a paraprofessional working in
 Day-Care/Preschool Program, 64-66
 First-Grade Program, 102-104
 Infant-Toddler Program, 42-44
 Kindergarten Program, 83-85
 Second-Grade Program, 122-124
 Third-Grade Program, 139-145

I

Instructional activities of a paraprofessional working in
 Day-Care/Preschool Program, 63
 First-Grade Program, 101-102
 Infant-Toddler Program, 40-41
 Kindergarten Program, 82-83
 Second-Grade Program, 120-121
 Third-Grade Program, 138-139

M

Motor Development
 Definition, 8-9, 157
Motor Development of children in
 Day-Care/Preschool Program, 61-62
 First-Grade Program, 100-101
 Infant-Toddler Program, 37-39
 Kindergarten Program, 81-82
 Second-Grade Program, 119-120
 Third-Grade Program, 137-138

N

Newton Study, 11
Noninstructional activities of a paraprofessional working in
  Day-Care/Preschool Program, 63-64
  First-Grade Program, 102
  Infant-Toddler Program, 41
  Kindergarten Program, 83
  Second-Grade Program, 121-122
  Third-Grade Program, 139
Nursery School Aides, 6

P

Perceptual Development
  Definition, 8, 158
Perceptual Development of children in
  Day-Care/Preschool Program, 60-61
  First-Grade Program, 99-100
  Infant-Toddler Program, 36-37
  Kindergarten Program, 80-81
  Second-Grade Program, 118-119
  Third-Grade Program, 136-137
Physical Development
  Definition, 9, 158
Physical Development of children in
  Day-Care/Preschool Program, 61-62
  First-Grade Program, 100-101
  Infant-Toddler Program, 37-39
  Kindergarten Program, 81-82
  Second-Grade Program, 119-120
  Third-Grade Program, 137-138
Preschool Assistants, 6

R

Rutgers Study, 11

S

Sensory Development
  Definition, 8, 158
Sensory Development of children in
  Day-Care/Preschool Program, 60-61
  First-Grade Program, 99-100
  Infant-Toddler Program, 36-37
  Kindergarten Program, 80-81
  Second-Grade Program, 118-119
  Third-Grade Program, 136-137
Special Child
  Definition, 17, 158
Stride Right Children's Center, 13
  Floor Plan, 14
  Playground Plan, 15

V

Volunteer Aides, 6
Volunteer Tutors, 6

Y

Yale-Fairfield Study, 11